DISCARD

PEOPLES *of*

NORTH AMERICA

VOLUME 5

Gypsies (Romany) – Irish

GROLIER

About This Book

Peoples of North America is a survey of the North American population at the start of the 21st century: the ethnic groups who make it up, their origins, culture, and lifestyle. The 10 volumes of the encyclopedia are organized alphabetically and describe all ethnic groups, from Afghans to West Africans. The peoples include well-established communities, relatively recent immigrants, and indigenous peoples who survive in significant numbers. Other entries also cover immigration-related and crosscultural subjects, such as inter-marriage, music, and race, to help you understand how different groups have contributed to shaping modern North America.

Each entry on a specific ethnic group explains who the people are and where they live, where they came from, how they lived in the past and how they live now, and their arts, culture, and politics. Fact files and maps show the states and cities where the major communities live today. The fact files also allow you to quickly find useful information, including population figures, immigration history, languages, dominant religions, typical jobs, national foods, typical names, famous individuals, and major community organizations. The statistical data are from the U.S. and Canadian censuses. Where no date is specified, the data are based on the latest available figures: the 2000 U.S. Census or the 1996 Canadian Census.

Entries on ethnic groups all contain a box listing useful websites. There are also special boxes giving detailed information about key people, events, places, cultures, or traditions. A "See also" box at the end of each entry points you to related articles elsewhere in the encyclopedia, allowing you to further investigate topics of interest.

The index covers all 10 volumes, so it will help you trace topics throughout the set. A glossary at the end of each book gives a brief explanation of important words and concepts, and a timeline provides a chronological account of key events in the history of immigration to North America.

First Published 2003 by Grolier,
an imprint of Scholastic Library Publishing,
Old Sherman Turnpike
Danbury, Connecticut 06816

© 2003 The Brown Reference Group plc

Set ISBN: 0–7172–5777–0
Volume 5 ISBN: 0–7172–5782–7

Library of Congress Cataloging-in-Publication Data

Peoples of North America
        p. cm.
    Includes indexes
    Summary: Profiles the native and immigrant groups that
have peopled North America, focusing on the modes and
monitoring of immigration.
    Contents: v. 1. Afghans-Bosnians – v. 2. Brazilians-Colombians –
v. 3. Colonial America-Egyptians – v. 4. Emigrés and refugees-
Guyanese – v. 5. Gypsies (Romany)-Irish – v. 6. Iroquois
confederacy-local politics, Canda – v. 7. Local politics, U.S.-Native
Americans, Southeast – v. 8. Native Americans, Southwest and
Mexico-Puerto Ricans – v. 9. Quebec separatism-social mobility and
race – v. 10. South Africans-World War II.
    ISBN 0-7172-5777-0 (set : alk. paper)
    1. Minorities – North America – Encyclopedias, Juvenile. 2.
Immigrants – North America – Encyclopedias, Juvenile. 3.
Ethnology – North America – Encyclopedias, Juvenile. 4. North
America – Population – Encyclopedias, Juvenile. 5. North America
– History – Encyclopedias, Juvenile. 6. North America – Ethnic
relations – Encyclopedias, Juvenile. [1. North America – Population
– Encyclopedias. 2. Ethnology – North America – Encyclopedias.]

E49.P467 2003
305.8'0097'03 – dc21

2003042395

For information address the publisher:
Grolier, Scholastic Library Publishing,
Old Sherman Turnpike, Danbury, Connecticut 06816

Printed and bound in Singapore

For The Brown Reference Group plc
Academic Consultants: Donald Avery, Professor, Department of
History, University of Western Ontario;
Margaret Connell-Szasz, Professor of Native American and Celtic
History, University of New Mexico
Editors: Rachel Bean, Andrew Campbell, Dennis Cove,
Felicity Crowe, Mark Fletcher, Lee Stacy
Designer: Dax Fullbrook
Picture Researcher: Becky Cox
Indexer: Kay Ollerenshaw
Managing Editor: Tim Cooke

CONTENTS

Gypsies (Romany)

The Romany, often referred to as Gypsies, are one of the most mysterious ethnic groups in the United States. According to estimates, there are between 500,000 and 1 million Romany in North America, yet public awareness of their existence is very low. There are several reasons for this. First, there is a tendency among the Romany to conceal their ethnic identity in official surveys and census statistics. Second, the census and immigration authorities have never kept official figures on them. Finally, the Romany have traditionally engaged in occupations that did not keep them in one place for long periods of time.

Origins and Migration

The Romany originated in northwestern India and are no strangers to persecution. Their homeland was attacked in the 11th century by Muslim invaders, and they left India for Persia (modern Iran), where they stayed for several generations. The next wave of migration occurred during the 13th and 14th centuries, when they moved from Persia into eastern Europe. By the end of the 15th century the Romany could be found as far west as Britain, as far north as Scandinavia, and as far south as Spain. The third major migration took place in the 19th and 20th centuries, when some Romany left Europe for North and South America, particularly to escape Nazi persecution during World War II. A fourth migration began after the fall of communism in Central and Eastern Europe in 1989, with the Romany leaving the former communist countries for Western Europe and North America.

Romany Culture

Romany life revolves around two concepts: the family and the clan. The family is at the heart of the culture and includes not only parents and children but also aunts, uncles, cousins, and various other relatives. The organization of the family is very patriarchal, meaning that the men hold the positions of power. The second unit of identification is the clan. The structure and organization of clans vary from group to group. Some clans are named after a common ancestor or the clan's founder. Others are identified by the country where they live, the dialect of Romany they speak, or the occupation of the males in the group.

The Romany do not have a common religion; instead, they usually adopt the dominant faith of the areas where they settle. Therefore Romany communities may have Roman Catholics, Protestants,

Music and dancing are an integral part of Romany culture. The women in this photograph are wearing traditional Romany costume of brightly colored skirts and scarfs.

Muslims, or Orthodox Christians among them. In addition to the "official" religion the Romany also believe in the supernatural, such as omens and curses. It is common for them to carry good luck charms and other objects thought to protect them from misfortune.

The Romany in the United States

There are four main Romany groups in North America: the Vlax, who were slaves in Romania until 1864; the Romanichals, also called "English travelers"; the Bashalde, or Hungarian-Slovak Romany, who arrived from Central and Eastern Europe in the 19th century; and the "new wave" Romany, mainly from Hungary, Poland, Romania, and the Czech Republic, who began arriving in North America toward the end of the 20th century, after the fall of communism triggered an increase in racially motivated attacks against minority groups. The Romany can be found in all states, but the largest concentrations are in New York, Virginia, Illinois, Texas, Massachusetts, and along the Pacific Coast. They live primarily in cities, with populations of around 10,000 in Chicago and 15,000 in Los Angeles. Although they have adapted to the industrialized, urban society of North America, and most now have permanent homes, the Romany have retained their cultural identity and have kept their traditional fondness for travel.

Gypsies or Romany?

When the Romany first arrived in Europe, most people thought they were from Turkey or Egypt since they came from the east. Therefore they became known as "Egyptians" or "Gyptians," which later became corrupted to "Gypsies." The name "Romany" (sometimes spelled "Romani" or shortened to "Roma") derives from the Persian word "dom," which means "person."

See also

- Anti-immigrant prejudice (Volume 1)
- Immigrant experience (Volume 5)
- Multiple ethnic origins (Volume 7)
- Religion (Volume 9)
- World War II (Volume 10)

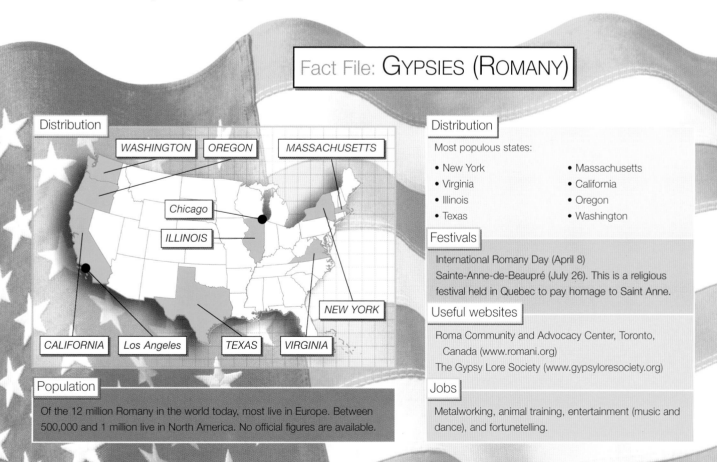

Fact File: GYPSIES (ROMANY)

Distribution

[Map of the United States with the following labels: WASHINGTON, OREGON, MASSACHUSETTS, Chicago, ILLINOIS, CALIFORNIA, Los Angeles, TEXAS, VIRGINIA, NEW YORK]

Distribution

Most populous states:

- New York
- Virginia
- Illinois
- Texas
- Massachusetts
- California
- Oregon
- Washington

Festivals

International Romany Day (April 8)
Sainte-Anne-de-Beaupré (July 26). This is a religious festival held in Quebec to pay homage to Saint Anne.

Useful websites

Roma Community and Advocacy Center, Toronto, Canada (www.romani.org)
The Gypsy Lore Society (www.gypsyloresociety.org)

Population

Of the 12 million Romany in the world today, most live in Europe. Between 500,000 and 1 million live in North America. No official figures are available.

Jobs

Metalworking, animal training, entertainment (music and dance), and fortunetelling.

Haida

Central Council of the Tlingit

The Central Council of the Tlingit and Haida Indian Tribes of Alaska (CCTHITA), based in Juneau, Alaska, represents over 24,000 Tlingit and Haida Indians and has a government-to-government relationship with the United States. Though the Haida and the Tlingit nations are two separate peoples, they chose to unite to affirm their sovereignty and preserve their traditional cermonies and other customs. The CCTHITA follows the ancient laws of both peoples.

See also

- Aleuts (Volume 1)
- Tlingits (Volume 10)

The Haida are one of the oldest traceable populations in North America, dating back at least 9,000 years. They live on the Queen Charlotte Islands, British Columbia, and Prince of Wales Island, Alaska. The Haida were once a seafaring tribe who survived by hunting seals and sea otters and fishing for salmon. Today their communities rely on commercial fishing and forestry for income.

Haida Traditions and Culture

The Haida were traditionally a warlike people who attacked other tribes for revenge, loot, and slaves. They were excellent woodcarvers and made objects such as ceremonial masks, totem poles, and 75-foot (25m) dugout canoes that could carry 40 people. Their most important ceremony was the potlatch, a lavish feast at which the host gave away or destroyed property to show off his wealth and status.

Europeans arrived in Haida territory in the late 18th century, bringing diseases that wiped out thousands of Haida. They set up fisheries that depleted the salmon population and overhunted sea otters for their fur. Over time the Haida abandoned their ceremonies and traditions and adapted to a new way of life. In 1980 the Haida Tribal Society was created to restore Haida culture and identity.

Fact File: HAIDA

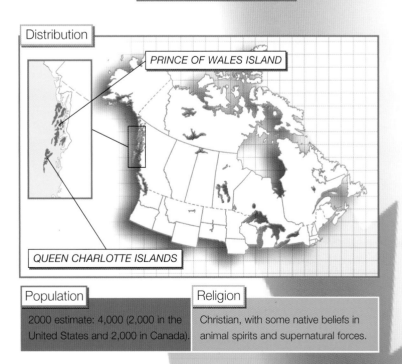

Distribution

PRINCE OF WALES ISLAND

QUEEN CHARLOTTE ISLANDS

Population

2000 estimate: 4,000 (2,000 in the United States and 2,000 in Canada).

Religion

Christian, with some native beliefs in animal spirits and supernatural forces.

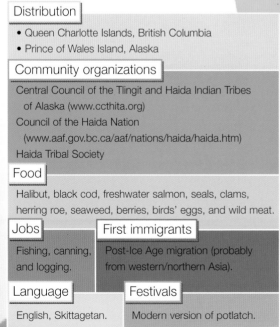

Distribution

- Queen Charlotte Islands, British Columbia
- Prince of Wales Island, Alaska

Community organizations

Central Council of the Tlingit and Haida Indian Tribes of Alaska (www.ccthita.org)
Council of the Haida Nation (www.aaf.gov.bc.ca/aaf/nations/haida/haida.htm)
Haida Tribal Society

Food

Halibut, black cod, freshwater salmon, seals, clams, herring roe, seaweed, berries, birds' eggs, and wild meat.

Jobs

Fishing, canning, and logging.

First immigrants

Post-Ice Age migration (probably from western/northern Asia).

Language

English, Skittagetan.

Festivals

Modern version of potlatch.

Haitians

Haitian Americans come from the world's first black republic, the Republic of Haiti, which is also the poorest nation in the Western Hemisphere. Haiti is located on the Caribbean island of Hispaniola and is extremely densely populated, with a population of about seven million people. Haitians have a long history of migration to the United States. Although the Haitian American community is well established and has many educated members working in the professions, Haitian Americans are still often stereotyped as poverty-stricken "boat people" who come to the United States solely as refugees.

History of Haitian Immigration

Haitian immigrants first came to the United States after the Haitian Revolution (1791–1803), when the black majority overthrew the ruling white minority in what was then a French colony. The French elite resettled in the French-speaking parts of the southern United States. Another major wave of Haitian immigration began in 1957, when a brutal dictator, "Papa Doc" Duvalier, came to power and drove out the country's professionals, merchants, and landowners. Duvalier was followed by his son, "Baby Doc," in the 1970s, and both educated and uneducated Haitians continued to flee to the United States and Canada.

When poor, black Creole-speaking Haitians wanted to leave, they could only afford to make the trip by boat. Tens of thousands of "boat people" tried to enter the United States illegally. Many drowned, and others were turned back by the U.S. Coast Guard or sent to the U.S. military base at Guantánamo Bay in Cuba. The temporary ousting of the democratically elected president, Jean-Bertrand Aristide, in September 1991 led to a new exodus of boat people. Since 1994, when the United States led a multinational peacekeeping force to occupy Haiti and put Aristide back in control, the U.S. government's policy has been to improve conditions on the island to stop emigration. The policy has not worked.

Haitian American Communities

The earliest Haitian Americans settled in cities such as New York and New Orleans. They were white, French-speaking, educated, wealthy professionals who assimilated well into both the American labor market and daily life. This pattern was repeated in the 20th century as Haiti's educated elite moved to New York City to escape from the Duvalier regime.

Voodoo

Haiti is the birthplace of a distinctive religion called "voodoo" (or "vodou"). When slaves from West Africa were taken to French colonial Haiti, they blended the Catholic beliefs of the French with their own faith, linking the saints with African gods and adding Catholic prayers to their singing, drumming, and dancing. Present-day voodoo emphasizes the importance of cooperating with an unseen spirit world. In a voodoo ceremony the priest or priestess (often wrongly called a "witch doctor") may enter a trance or sacrifice an animal in order to please the spirits. Voodoo is often seen as mysterious and sinister, but in fact it is open to anyone who asks to be initiated, regardless of race or nationality, and there is no need to renounce other religions, since voodoo may be practiced along with another faith.

Haitian refugees, or "boat people," sail to the Florida Keys. When they land, they will be taken into custody while the government considers their request for asylum.

Distribution

Most populous cities:
- Miami
- Montreal
- New York City
- Chicago
- New Orleans
- Los Angeles
- Boston

Chicago

New York City

Los Angeles

Boston

Miami

New Orleans

Region of origin

Haiti

The country of Haiti occupies the western third of the island of Hispaniola in the Caribbean.

Population

U.S.: over 500,000 (2000 census estimate; true figure unknown because of high rate of illegal immigration).

Language

French and Haitian Creole (a distinct language that arose from the fusion of French with West African languages).

Dates of major arrivals

- 1957–1986: "Papa Doc" and "Baby Doc" Duvalier dictatorships.
- 1991: During the temporary ousting of President Aristide.

Useful websites

EchodHaiti.com (www.echodhaiti.com)
National Coalition for Haitian Rights (www.nchr.org)
Haitian American Grassroots Coalition
  (http://hagcoaliltion.freehosting.net)
The Haitian Times (www.haitiantimes.com)
Sacred Arts of Haitian Vodou (American Museum of Natural History)
  (www.amnh.org/exhibitions/vodou)
Haiti Global Village (www.haitiglobalvillage.com)
Kreyol.com (http://kreyol.com)
Official Haitian Carnival Website (www.kanaval.com)
Discover Haiti (www.discoverhaiti.com)

Notable Haitian Americans

John James Audubon, wildlife artist.
Edwidge Danticat, poet and novelist.
Wyclef Jean, hip-hop and rap artist.
Pierre Toussaint, ex-slave hairdresser who became a successful
  entrepreneur and philanthropist.

Community organizations

Haitian Refugee Center, Miami.
Haitian American Chamber of Commerce, Miami.

Religion

Mostly Catholic; many people also practice voodoo.

Festivals

All major Christian festivals including Christmas Day and Easter.
New Year's Day.
Carnival or Kanaval (February).
Independence Day (January 1).
Discovery of Haiti Day (December 5).

Food

Riz et pois colles (kidney beans and rice) and *kabrit boukannen ak bon pima* (barbecued goat with hot pepper).

The Upper West Side was the first stop for migrants, who then moved on to Brooklyn and Queens. However, these more recent arrivals faced more prejudice and found it harder to fit in. At the end of the 20th century Florida became the top destination for Haitian immigrants. Some of New York's Haitian Americans also started relocating to Miami and Montreal.

No matter where they are located, all Haitian American communities revolve around the family. Most people spend their free time with their family and friends. Children stay at home until they marry, and elderly parents are cared for within the family. Haitian women tend to have more freedom in the United States than at home, particularly when they work. They keep in close contact with relatives in Haiti, and many send money back home on a regular basis. Underemployment is a serious problem for Haitian Americans. Many of the less-educated work in service and labor industries, and large numbers of illegal immigrants find work in cash jobs.

Carnival, an annual festival similar to Mardi Gras, is a major event in Haiti. Haitian Americans mark the occasion with events like this dance party in a restaurant in Miami.

Haitian Culture

Perhaps as a result of the prejudice many Haitian Americans have faced, the Haitian American community guards its culture closely. In New York and Miami, where Haitian neighborhoods have grown up on the Upper West Side and in North Miami respectively, many Haitian businesses cater to the local community's practical and cultural needs. In addition, there are weekly Haitian newspapers, local radio shows, and Haitian American programming on cable TV stations.

Haitian Americans celebrate several holidays and festivals during the year, and they mark these occasions by cooking special Haitian dishes, such as *kabrit boukannen ak bon pima* (barbecued goat with hot pepper). On New Year's Eve they eat black-eyed-pea patties for good luck. Other traditional Haitian foods that remain popular today include *riz et pois colles* (kidney beans and rice) and *riz djon-djon* (rice with black mushrooms).

Those Haitian immigrants who come to the United States from rural areas of Haiti bring with them their faith in voodoo, a blend of Roman Catholicism and West African religions. Another important part of life for many people is traditional Haitian medicine. Folk healers study the spirits and use medicinal plants and voodoo ceremonies to heal their patients. In Haitian neighborhoods it is possible to buy herbal remedies from Haitian pharmacists.

Politics

During the harsh dictatorships of the Duvalier family (1957–1986) New York City was at the heart of Haitian opposition. In 1968 the Haitian American community began to organize to lobby the U.S. government on issues of concern. In recent years the Miami Haitian community has become more involved in local politics. In 2000 a Haitian American was elected mayor of North Miami, and in 2002 the district had a Haitian American majority council.

See also

Hawaiians

Hawaii is a chain of islands in the Pacific Ocean located 2,500 miles southwest of the North American mainland. The islands are actually the tips of volcanoes, some of which remain active. The original settlers of the Hawaiian islands were eastern Polynesians, probably from the Marquesas Islands, who arrived by canoe around A.D. 300. The population of the islands reached almost 300,000 before the arrival of Captain James Cook in 1778. The European sailors brought diseases that killed many native inhabitants, and by the 1850s 75 percent of the population had been wiped out. Today, although the number of native Hawaiians has risen, Hawaiians have had to work hard to maintain their language, culture, and religion.

The Road to Statehood

During the late 18th century Hawaii became a provisioning point for merchant ships and a center for Pacific whaling, and native men were recruited as crew by visiting vessels. The first missionaries arrived in the 1820s and soon began to undermine traditional religion and culture. Many Hawaiian men immigrated to the U.S. mainland during the California Gold Rush of the 1840s and 1850s, while others went to the Pacific Northwest as fur traders, sailors, and fishermen.

By the mid-1800s plantation agriculture was established in Hawaii, and a shortage of local labor led to the recruitment of workers from China, Japan, the Philippines, and Portugal. In 1898 Hawaii was annexed by the United States, and a military base was established at Pearl Harbor. Hawaii became a major tourist destination after World War II (1939–1945) and was declared the 50th U.S. state in 1959.

Hawaiian Culture and Community

The spirit of "aloha" is vital to Hawaiian culture. This one word can be used to convey various meanings, including hello, goodbye, peace, and welcome. Native Hawaiians place a high value on family life and prefer to invest in social relations and family networks rather than pursuing individual material wealth.

Because Hawaiians have always been willing to interact with other racial and ethnic groups, mainstream Hawaiian culture is now a mixture of traditional native practices and the diverse cultures of more recent immigrants. Hawaii has the highest rate of intermarriage within the United States. The diversity of immigration is also reflected in local cuisine, with a range of Japanese, Portuguese, Chinese, and Korean dishes now considered everyday fare. A wide variety of religions are practiced in the state; residents of Hawaii may be Catholic, Protestant (especially Mormon), Buddhist, Shintoist, Hindu, Jewish, or Muslim.

Polynesian culture is the foundation of many Hawaiian art forms. These Polynesian dancers are performing on a boat at the Polynesian Cultural Center on Oahu, Hawaii.

The Hawaiian language is a branch of the Eastern Polynesian languages of the South Pacific. Before European contact there was no written form of Hawaiian, and history was passed down through oral storytelling. Today the spoken language is declining, with fewer than 9,000 people now fluent, although Hawaiian was declared an official state language in 1978 and is now taught in some schools.

Traditional activities such as surfing, hula dancing, the making of "leis" (flower necklaces), and canoe racing regained popularity in the 20th century. The ancient Hawaiian religion has also enjoyed a revival. It recognizes hundreds of deities and is based on the concepts of *ul mana* (spiritual power) and *kapu* (taboos or ritual avoidance).

Native Hawaiians and Land Rights

Appropriation of native land and annexation by the United States have both had a devastating effect on native Hawaiians. During the 1840s, when the traditional form of communal property ownership was abolished, most land was appropriated by the king, chiefs, and government, and eventually fell under the control of plantation owners. Today land rights are a major issue, with demands for territory controlled by the government or by private individuals of non-Hawaiian descent to be returned to the native population.

Luaus

On special occasions Hawaiians hold elaborate, festive banquets called "luaus." At a luau a pig is roasted in an earth oven with hot rocks and served with other dishes such as yams, chicken, *lomi* (marinated salmon), and cakes. Guests are also treated to traditional music and dances such as "hula," an ancient dance rooted in the mythology of Hawaii.

See also

- Intermarriage (Volume 5)
- Music (Volume 7)
- Native peoples and land rights (Volume 8)
- Pacific Islanders (Volume 8)

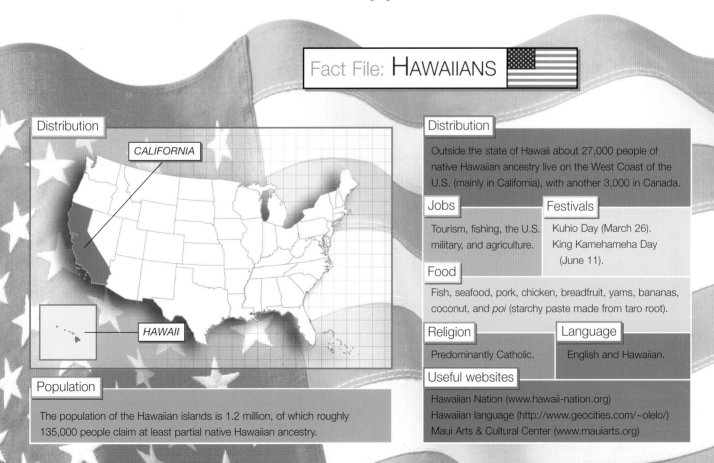

Fact File: HAWAIIANS

Distribution

CALIFORNIA

HAWAII

Population

The population of the Hawaiian islands is 1.2 million, of which roughly 135,000 people claim at least partial native Hawaiian ancestry.

Distribution

Outside the state of Hawaii about 27,000 people of native Hawaiian ancestry live on the West Coast of the U.S. (mainly in California), with another 3,000 in Canada.

Jobs

Tourism, fishing, the U.S. military, and agriculture.

Festivals

Kuhio Day (March 26).
King Kamehameha Day (June 11).

Food

Fish, seafood, pork, chicken, breadfruit, yams, bananas, coconut, and *poi* (starchy paste made from taro root).

Religion

Predominantly Catholic.

Language

English and Hawaiian.

Useful websites

Hawaiian Nation (www.hawaii-nation.org)
Hawaiian language (http://www.geocities.com/~olelo/)
Maui Arts & Cultural Center (www.mauiarts.org)

Useful websites

National Center of Complementary
and Alternative Medicine
(http://nccam.nih.gov/nccam)
Portal for a variety of subjects
associated with religion and
spirituality, including voodoo and
rootwork (http://dmoz.org/
Society/Religion_and_Spirituality)
Portal to the websites of a number
of health initiatives and activities
of the U.S. Department of Health
and Human Services and other
federal departments and agencies
(www.hhs.gov)

*A Chinese herbalist mixing
treatments in his store in San
Francisco, California. Chinese
herbalists practice in virtually every
Chinatown in the United States.*

The maintenance of good health and the treatment of illness are fundamental to human life. Different peoples throughout the world have to determine how to deal with issues about health, sickness, mental illness, and death; their attitudes and methods reflect their own cultural values, traditions, and patterns of social behavior. Beliefs about health generally fall into two categories: preventing illness and treating illness. Often such beliefs include both physical treatments, such as drugs, herbs, massage, and surgery, and psychological treatments, such as rituals and therapies in which patients talk about their problems. In the United States, which is home to an immensely ethnically diverse population, many different approaches to health and healing exist alongside one another. However, the dominant approach, and that of the American healthcare system, is based on the Western scientific tradition of medicine.

Blending Traditions

Ethnic groups often arrive in the United States with a developed set of beliefs about health based on the medical culture in their homeland. These beliefs are then mixed, at some level, with the Western belief in scientific medical practices. The exact mixture of these two belief systems can vary between individuals, families, and ethnic groups. Later generations may maintain home or folk remedies, even if Western medicine also provides a cure. First- and second-generation immigrants may ignore Western prescriptions or misuse them. Generally, they remain more comfortable with the remedies and medical care they used before immigration. Non-European and poor European immigrants tend to retain traditional remedies through more generations than their wealthier European counterparts.

Folk Healthcare

Folk medicine uses diet, herbs, patent medicines, incantations, charms, and healing rituals to bring healing and health. Often, not only the patient and healer are involved, but the whole family of the patient and the community in which they live. The complexity of America's folk medical heritage and practitioners is a result of the diversity of immigrants and native peoples, as well as their many ways of dealing with health questions. Many folk healthcare systems are based on indigenous folk healers who specialize in diagnosing "illnesses." Examples are the Mexican *curanderos* ("curers"), Latin American *espirtistas* ("spiritualists"), African rootworkers (healers who practice rootwork, a blend of African, Native American, and European spiritual beliefs and folk practices so named because of the prominent role of dried roots in rituals), as well as herbalists and faith healers from many different cultures.

Native American health practices vary from tribe to tribe, but virtually all groups believe in the harmony of the supernatural and natural worlds with human beings. Any disruption in this harmony is thought to cause misfortune and sickness. The Native Americans developed an extensive collection of cures and remedies, many so effective that they influenced Western medicine and continue to be widely used. Today many Native American tribes still practice medicine in the traditional manner.

Immigrant Traditions

African Americans arrived in North America bearing a wealth of distinctive health beliefs and practices. However, their forced dispersal as slaves undermined their practice of medicine in the United States, although African slaves in the Caribbean did maintain the traditions of their homelands. African folk medicine includes the belief that malevolent magic causes illness. The most common forms of magic used to counter sickness are voodoo and rootwork. These practices continue to be used throughout the Caribbean and have been adopted in parts of the United States, especially by poor African Americans in rural and inner-city areas.

Another important medical tradition introduced to North America is Chinese medicine, which in recent years has also attracted Americans with no Chinese ancestry. Chinese medicine stresses harmony with nature and balance in all things, and is based on the complementary concepts of yin and yang, the five elements (wood, fire, earth, metal, and water), and the concept of *chi* (the body's energy force). It emphasizes diet and prevention of illness using acupuncture, herbs, massage, and exercise to focus the body's natural curative powers. Chinese folk healers are advisers, rather than authorities, and treat patients individually based on their constitutions and life situations. The emphasis on natural cures, the "holistic" approach in which the healer examines wider aspects of lifestyle, and the apparent success in treating conditions such as the skin complaint eczema have led to an increase in the popularity of Chinese medicine.

Northern Europeans arrived in America with the beliefs and practices common in Europe when they left. Their ideas on illness and remedies were based on ancient Greek medicine, principally the teachings of Galen, which shaped European professional and folk medicine for centuries. This tradition was based on the idea of humors, four liquids in the body that were believed to determine people's temperament, health,

Medical examinations

When different immigrant groups attempted to enter the United States in the late 19th and early 20th centuries, they had to undergo rigorous medical examinations. The two main entry points were Ellis Island in New York for European immigrants and San Francisco for Asian immigrants. The American medical inspectors often applied stereotypes to immigrants, equating the Irish with cholera, the Chinese with bubonic plague, and Jews with tuberculosis. Doctors from these and other immigrant groups were able to intervene and challenge the U.S. medical officials' prejudices.

A voodoo priestess performing a ritual in New Orleans, Louisiana.

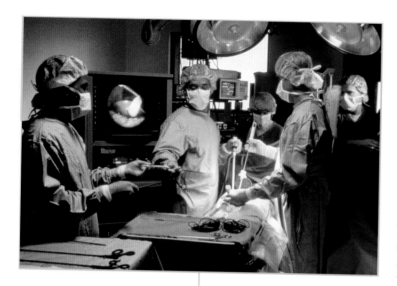

A surgical team performing an operation on a patient in a hospital in San Diego, California.

Korean healthcare survey

In 1990 a survey conducted at California State University, Los Angeles, found that educated and assimilated Korean immigrants are as likely, or even more likely, to use traditional medicine than Koreans in lower socioeconomic groups. It suggests that only Koreans with medical insurance and higher incomes can afford to use traditional folk healers. Since folk healers are not covered by insurance, the higher income is necessary to pay the additional bills. This finding runs counter to the accepted notion that only lower socioeconomic groups use traditional healers.

and appearance. Doctors thought illness was a result of an imbalance in the humors. Common remedies included bloodletting and sweating to remove excess heat, poultices to draw out impurities, and diet and exercise to balance the body. Combined with Native American remedies, these ideas form the basis for a large portion of the popular health practices in America today, such as purgatives, health foods, and tonics.

The American Health System

In general terms, Western medical science is more objective than many of the folk medicines practiced in the United States. It focuses on the biological explanation and treatment of illness—as opposed to viewing it in religious, spiritual, or cultural terms—and denies the influence of any supernatural forces. Western medicine and the American healthcare system are based on scientific beliefs and practices related to health and healing. Heath professionals such as doctors, nurses, chiropractors, osteopaths, and other licensed providers receive formal training in universities and medical schools and deliver care in clinics and hospitals. While maintaining folk remedies for many less serious health problems, most Americans turn to conventional Western medicine to treat serious illnesses.

Healthcare in America continues to change rapidly. Only 25 years ago most people had indemnity insurance coverage, which allowed the patient to choose any doctor, hospital, or provider. The insurance and patient would then each pay part of the bill. Today more than half of Americans are part of some type of managed healthcare plan. The three main types are preferred provider plans (PPOs), health maintenance organizations (HMOs), and point of service (POS) plans. Each of these plans provides access to conventional healthcare doctors, hospitals, and other providers for a set rate or percentage of the overall billing.

The mainstream health system in the United States does not provide traditional ethnic treatments at this time, and most insurance providers will not support visits to folk medicine providers. Doctors are trained to be impersonal and scientific in their analysis of disease. Ethnic groups often describe conventional doctors as cold or uncaring, especially when compared to their folk healers. Some progress has been made recently in making conventional healthcare systems and providers more responsive to ethnic groups; however, a great divide continues to separate the two spheres of medicine.

Hispanic Americans

The term "Hispanic" refers to anyone originating in Central or South America, or claiming Spanish ancestry. Hispanic Americans have had an important influence on the culture of the United States, from the introduction of foods like tacos and tortillas, to their work in entertainment, business, sports, science, and the military. Hispanics are one of the fastest-growing groups in America—currently 13 percent of the total population. As such their vote has significant weight in elections and, in 2000, helped George W. Bush win the presidency. Certain Hispanic groups tend to live together in certain regions. For example, 64 percent of Puerto Ricans live in the northeastern states and 80 percent of Cubans are situated in the south. Nearly half of all Hispanics live in urban areas. Overall, the group is young, with 35.7 percent of Hispanic Americans under 18 years old.

Education statistics for Hispanic groups vary widely. For example, in 2000, 23 percent of Cubans held a bachelor's degree, while only 6.9 percent of Mexican Hispanics had the same qualification. Hispanic Americans are more likely to be unemployed than non-Hispanics. Those who do work tend to be found in service positions and, in general, earning less than non-Hispanic workers in the same positions. Due to these factors Hispanics in the United States are more likely to be living below the poverty level than non-Hispanic people.

Fact File: HISPANIC AMERICANS

Distribution

CALIFORNIA · ILLINOIS · NEW YORK · NEW JERSEY · ARIZONA · NEW MEXICO · TEXAS · FLORIDA

Population

U.S.: 35,305,818 (2000 census).

Most populous states

California, Texas, New Mexico, Arizona, Illinois, New York, New Jersey, and Florida.

Festivals

All major Roman Catholic festivals.
Easter Blessing of the Animals (Spring).
The Day of the Dead (November 1–2).

Food

Tortillas, beans, guacamole, salsa, tamales, and tequila.

Jobs

19.4% work in service occupations; 14% work in professional occupations; 11.6% work as laborers.

Community organizations

The Hispanic-American community has so many organizations that the reader is referred to www.fundsnetservices.com/latorg.htm

Names

Common Hispanic surnames include García, Martínez, Rodríguez, López, Hernández, González, Pérez, Sánchez, Rivera, Ramírez, Torres, and Gómez.

Hondurans

Politics

As a comparatively recent immigrant group, Honduran Americans, along with other Central Americans, have been lobbying for improved rights for undocumented workers. The action group Aliens for Better Immigration Law was formed in 1994 to help immigrants gain the right to work while awaiting their green cards. Legal Honduran migrants are gradually taking on U.S. citizenship in order to get more involved in politics.

Honduran Americans moved to the United States in greater numbers between 1980 and 2000 than in previous decades. Between 1980 and 1990 some 34,220 Hondurans migrated to the United States. The U.S. Census shows that by 2000 there were an estimated 217,569 Honduran Americans in the United States.

The earliest Honduran Americans settled in New York City and other traditional centers for Hispanic migration, such as Los Angeles, California, and Miami, Florida. Today, according to the 2000 census, southern Florida has taken over from New York as the number-one destination for Honduran Americans. However, although there are still large concentrations on the coasts, Honduran Americans are now spread throughout most of the United States.

The Hondurans are an ethnically diverse group that includes Maya Indians, Spanish, Africans, and black Caribs, known as Garifuna. The Garifuna Hondurans tend to base themselves in New York and to associate with other members of the Garifuna-speaking community, largely from Belize. Spanish-speaking Hondurans mix with other members of the established Latino community.

Since the Honduran American community is relatively new, many of its members work in unskilled jobs and are not, with the exception of the Garifuna, easily discernible from other Hispanics. There are significant numbers of illegal Honduran immigrants who keep a low profile in order to avoid deportation.

Waves of Migration

Honduran Americans come from the small country of Honduras in Central America. Slightly larger than the state of Tennessee, with a population of about six million people, the country has both Pacific and Atlantic coastlines. The earliest migrants fled Honduras during the unstable transition to independence from Spain in 1821. However, most immigration to the United States occurred after 1956, when political upheaval led to a military takeover of Honduras, and the country was destabilized as military and civilian groups struggled for power. Immigration to the United States increased in the 1980s, when civil wars in neighboring Central American countries threatened to spill over into Honduras. Changes in U.S. immigration law in 1986 also increased the number of Hondurans moving to the United States because illegal immigrants saw a new opportunity to

Honduran Americans have strong ties to their native country; when Hurricane Mitch hit Honduras in 1998, they raised money and sent disaster relief to the victims.

gain legal status. As the economic situation in Honduras failed to improve—with 53 percent living below the poverty line (in 1993) and an unemployment rate of 28 percent (in 2000)—more Hondurans continued to move north throughout the 1990s.

Honduran Communities in North America

The Garifuna live largely in New York and have their own separate community with their own foods, language, and music. Unlike Spanish-speaking Hondurans, the Garifuna have a long history of their men working away from their families for extended periods. Spanish-speaking Honduran families tend to resemble the traditional American family, with a similar number of divorces and children. Soccer is a major part of their social life; they follow their national team and have formed soccer leagues with other Central Americans.

It is typically easier for Honduran American girls to gain higher education than for boys because boys are expected to start work as soon as possible to contribute to the family's income. Finding work can be difficult for Honduran Americans, since many are undocumented workers. Those with legal papers often work in unskilled jobs. However, there are professional Honduran Americans, as the Honduran American Physicians' Association demonstrates.

Notable Honduran Americans

Miguel A. Estrada, judge, District of Columbia Circuit Court of Appeals.
Julio Melera, journalist and magazine publisher.
Neida Sandoval, host of *Despierta América* (Univisión cable network).

See Also

- Belizeans (Volume 1)
- Hispanic Americans (Volume 5)
- Immigration legislation (Volume 5)
- Mayans (Volume 7)
- Nicaraguans (Volume 8)
- Salvadorans (Volume 9)
- Spanish (Volume 10)

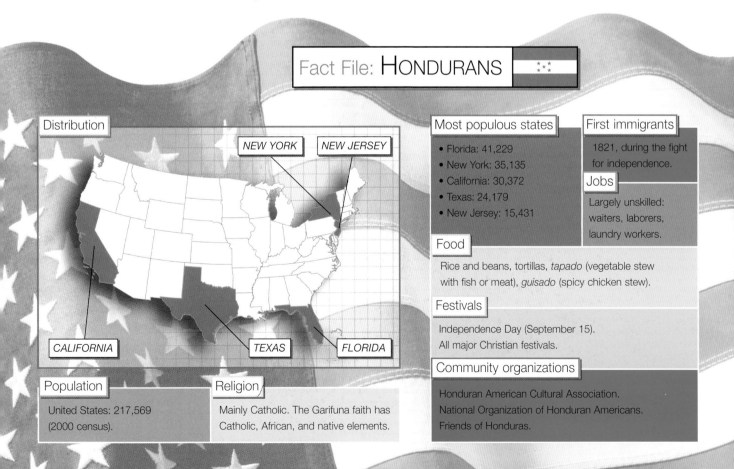

Fact File: HONDURANS

Distribution

NEW YORK NEW JERSEY

CALIFORNIA TEXAS FLORIDA

Population

United States: 217,569 (2000 census).

Religion

Mainly Catholic. The Garifuna faith has Catholic, African, and native elements.

Most populous states

- Florida: 41,229
- New York: 35,135
- California: 30,372
- Texas: 24,179
- New Jersey: 15,431

Food

Rice and beans, tortillas, *tapado* (vegetable stew with fish or meat), *guisado* (spicy chicken stew).

Festivals

Independence Day (September 15). All major Christian festivals.

Community organizations

Honduran American Cultural Association. National Organization of Honduran Americans. Friends of Honduras.

First immigrants

1821, during the fight for independence.

Jobs

Largely unskilled: waiters, laborers, laundry workers.

Housing

Housing not only provides shelter for people, it also creates an essential part of their environment. It is shaped by natural and climatic factors, such as the local availability of building materials like wood, stone, and clay for bricks, and whether the house has to protect its inhabitants from extreme heat or cold, high winds, or heavy rain. Equally importantly, housing is influenced by the people who make and live in it, by their family structure, social customs, traditions, and wealth. Housing in North America has always reflected the natural and environmental contrasts of the vast continent, as well as the diverse cultural and ethnic groups that make up its population.

Early North American Housing

The variety of housing in North America results from the combined influence of environmental and social factors. Early European settlers recreated the housing they were used to in their homeland, using the materials they found in North America. The English and Dutch settlers built wooden frame houses up and down the eastern seaboard, and Scandinavian and German settlers constructed different varieties of log cabins. Pioneers on the Midwest prairies built houses from turf called "sod shanties," and Spanish settlers in the Southwest used adobe brick construction that combined Native American and European building methods.

The lifestyle of people influenced their housing. On the Great Plains the Sioux and other nomadic Native American peoples made tepees from buffalo hides. These structures could easily be dismantled, transported, and reerected as the tribes moved around. Along the cold northwest coast Native Americans built cedar-plank houses. In New England coastal towns seafaring men built "widow's walks," or fenced-in walkways, on flat portions of roofs, from which wives and families could watch for the return of their men's ships.

Climate also influenced the evolution of North American housing. Early farms in New England had a series of buildings attaching the farmhouse to the barn so that the farmers could stay mostly inside during the bitter winters. Southern settlers built kitchens around the back of the house to avoid the heat of the cookstove. Southern homes also boasted a front porch. Historians believe porches may have come from the African American "shotgun" house, which has its roots in West Africa and the Caribbean. A shotgun house is a modest building, one room wide, one story high, and several rooms deep, with windows on only the narrow front and

A Crow Indian tepee on the Great Plains made from buffalo hides stretched over a wooden frame.

back of the house—there was no point in having windows down the side walls since the space between shotgun houses was so small—and the main entrance on the narrow street front. Although porches spread to all parts of North America, in the south they were a particularly important social gathering area. In colder northern climates people tended to congregate inside.

Urban Immigrant Neighborhoods

After the Industrial Revolution of the early 19th century most of the immigrants who flocked to work in urban areas in North America could not afford to build their own homes and had to rent substandard housing. Because of this unprecedented population explosion— New York's population alone expanded by 800 percent between the War of 1812 and the beginning of the Civil War in 1861—entrepreneurs converted existing homes and entire city blocks into apartments. They designed these apartments, called tenements, specifically for dense, low-cost rental housing. The first was built in 1833. Tenements were infamous for their overcrowding and unsanitary, dark, damp conditions that bred disease. In New York City Irish and German immigrants were the first to live in tenements. After complaints by health officials and housing reformers such as writer Jacob Riis governments enacted a series of reforms to address the health hazards of overcrowded tenements.

Tenements on the Lower East Side, New York City, built in the 19th century to house immigrants who flocked to the city in search of work.

On a brighter note, crowded neighborhoods often created close-knit communities that maintained important aspects of traditional ethnic culture. Some immigrant neighborhoods became famous enclaves, with names reflecting their ethnic composition, such as "Chinatown" in New York and San Francisco, "Little Italy" in New York, and "Sonoratown," as early 20th-century Los Angeles called its Mexican community. Similar areas across the country created networks to help immigrants move within North America. However, these neighborhoods also isolated various ethnic groups, which often led to mistrust between people of different races and religious backgrounds.

North American industry also produced mass-housing projects outside large urban areas. Thousands of shotgun-style mill houses appeared around the numerous textile mills in smaller towns and cities. In rural areas mining towns—found everywhere from the coalfields of Appalachia to the copper- and silvermines of the West— sprang up with small shacks owned by the mining companies.

In the 20th century tenements eventually gave way to public housing funded by federal and state governments. These "projects" housed a disproportionate number of impoverished black and

Log cabins

A symbol of the American frontier, the log cabin was a natural housing choice on the heavily forested lands of North America. Swedish and Finnish settlers brought their log cabin construction techniques to the Delaware River valley as early as 1638. The Swedes shaped the logs along their length—curving their upper side and carving out a concave shape along their lower edge—so that the logs fitted tightly together. German immigrants, who also built log cabins, did not fit the logs together edge to edge, but filled the gaps between them with materials like clay and horsehair.

A Hindu shrine in the kitchen of an Asian Indian American family in Philadelphia, Pennsylvania.

The kitchen

The kitchen has long been the social center of most low-income immigrants' homes. These families have traditionally preferred large eat-in kitchens to the arrangement embraced by many middle-income American families, with a small, utilitarian kitchen and separate dining room. In early immigrant families women often did housework or sewed piecework while visiting and socializing in the kitchen. Italian women in particular did their housework together, keeping the vestiges of a shared housekeeping system called *cortile*.

See also

- Architecture (Volume 1)
- Cities, U.S. (Volume 2)
- Ghettos (Volume 4)
- Reservation system (Volume 9)
- Urban reform and race (volume 10)

Hispanic people. The buildings often became plagued by gangs, drugs, violence, and racial isolation. By the year 2000 city councils had demolished some huge housing projects, such as Chicago's Lakefront Properties, that they considered to be beyond redemption.

Making a House a Home

Ethnic neighborhoods in urban areas encouraged strong, cohesive communities by daily interaction among family and neighbors. The front porch and sidewalk were important places of social interaction. Immigrants also had to adapt their cultural habits to new living conditions. A writer in early 20th-century New York noticed a lot of shouting back and forth in an Italian neighborhood as mothers, from windows above, supervised their children playing below. Since close supervision of children was essential in Italian culture, these mothers were adapting to their new environment as best they could.

While many immigrants may never realize their dream of owning their own home, they do seek to use and decorate it in their own way. In the 20th century many immigrants from Cambodia furnished their houses with American-style furniture with the exception of one room, in which they simply covered the floor with mats in the manner of their homeland. In many immigrants' homes wall decorations include images of their home country or religious icons. Altars and altar rooms are also prevalent, particularly among Cuban, Mexican, and Asian Indian communities. Italian families often move arrangements of holy items, kept traditionally in the bedroom, to the kitchen. For most low-income immigrants the kitchen is the social center of the home.

Fragmentation of Urban Immigrant Communities

As second-generation immigrants and their descendants begin to earn higher wages, they often move to newer neighborhoods on the outskirts of cities where they can afford their own homes. While providing more space and privacy, these new neighborhoods often fragment families—instead of daily interactions, they see each other only during visits. However, the new homeowners can also grow in their gardens the traditional foods from their homeland, or they can make part of their home available to other family members. Although these moves follow the American dream of upward mobility and home ownership, many immigrants and their descendants have also found that they involve a certain degree of isolation from their families and communities.

Hungarians

It is difficult to determine the exact number of Hungarians who have come to North America. Until 1918 Hungary was a multiethnic region of the Austro-Hungarian empire; and when immigrants from the area arrived in the United States, customs officials often recorded them as Hungarians or Magyars without making a distinction. Magyars are the dominant ethnic group in Hungary; but after World War I (1914–1918) Hungary was carved up, and its borders no longer included some areas where Magyars lived. In the early part of the 1900s waves of poverty-stricken Hungarians arrived in the United States, and many Americans incorrectly identified them as gypsies or Mongols. Following the unsuccessful Hungarian Revolution in 1956, in which rebels attempted to overthrow the country's communist government, Hungarians received more coverage in the North American press, and earlier misconceptions largely disappeared. Today Hungarians are well assimilated in American society. Unless families are particularly dedicated to maintaining a dual identity, most American-born Hungarians have only a passing knowledge of their Hungarian ancestry and language. However, this trend is less evident in areas like New York, Cleveland, and Chicago, where greater numbers of Hungarians live and maintain more distinct communities.

Hungarian refugees arriving in New York in 1957. Following the unsuccessful Hungarian Revolution of 1956, some 38,000 Hungarians fled the communist regime in their homeland for the United States.

Hungarians in the United States, like many other immigrants from eastern Europe, settled mainly around large industrial centers. The 2000 U.S. Census estimated the population of Hungarian Americans to be 942,993. In 1996 the Hungarian population in Canada was 24,650, with the majority living in Ontario.

Early Immigrants

The first Hungarians to arrive in the United States came during colonial times. They were not part of a mass immigration, but were individuals, mainly men, who were explorers, missionaries, and adventurers. By the 1840s Hungarian scholars also began arriving in North America. They wrote about their experiences in books and journals, which encouraged others to follow.

A major wave of immigration was prompted by the unsuccessful revolution of Magyar leaders against their Austrian overlords in 1848. Hungary had been part of the Austrian empire since the beginning of

Useful websites

Hungarian American Coalition
(www.hungary.com/hac)
Hungarian folk culture in America
(www.hunmagyar.org/)
Hungarian American Chamber of
Commerce of New England
(www.hungary.com/haccne/)
Hungarian American folk tales
(www.sru.edu/depts/library/imc/
FolkTales/magarac.htm)
Hungarian Human Rights
Foundation (www.hhrf.org/)

Fact File: HUNGARIANS

Distribution

- Most populous states:
Pennsylvania, Illinois, Ohio, New Jersey,
and New York. Also significant groups
in Michigan, Connecticut, Wisconsin,
Indiana, West Virginia, and Ontario.

- Most populous cities:
The industrial/coal areas such as
Pittsburgh, Chicago, Cleveland,
Philadelphia, New York City,
and Toronto.

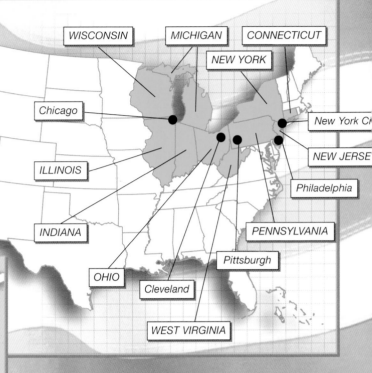

WISCONSIN | MICHIGAN | CONNECTICUT
NEW YORK
Chicago
New York C₁
ILLINOIS
NEW JERSE
Philadelphia
INDIANA
PENNSYLVANIA
Pittsburgh
OHIO
Cleveland
WEST VIRGINIA

Region of origin

Hungary

Hungary in eastern Europe.

Population

U.S.: 942,993 (2000 census); Canada: 24,650 (1996 census).

Language

Hungarian is spoken at home by the most recent wave of
immigrants who have arrived in America from World War II
onward. It is classified as Finno-Ugric and is part of the Ural-
Altaic language group. This body of languages is called
"agglutinative," which means that it is possible to take one
word and turn it into a complex phrase by adding prefixes
and suffixes to it.

Dates of major arrivals

- 1849: "Forty-Niners," supporters of the failed 1848 revolution for
Hungarian independence, who fled their Austro-Hungarian overlords.
- 1880s–1914: the "Great Economic Migration," about 1.7 million
impoverished Hungarians came to the United States in search of
work before World War I.
- 1956: Some 38,000 "Fifty-Sixers" fled to the United States after their
failed attempt to overthrow the communist government.

Community organizations

The Hungarian American Coalition
(www.hungary.com/hac) works to
promote and unify the Hungarian
American community in the
United States.

First immigrants

The first Hungarian
immigrants to the United
States came during colonial
times. They were often
explorers, missionaries,
and adventurers.

Names

Common surnames: Nagy, Kovacs (meaning "smith"), Toth, Szabo
("tailor"), Horvath, Kiss.

Famous individuals

Béla Bartók, composer.
George Soros, billionaire businessman.

Religion

Mainly Roman Catholic, as well as significant numbers of
Protestants (mainly Calvinist and Lutheran).

Festivals

- March 15 (marking the 1848 Revolution).
- August 20 (St. Stephen's Day—patron saint of Hungary).
- October 23 (marking the 1956 Revolution).

Food

Substantial meat dishes flavored with paprika and garlic are
typical of Hungarian cuisine. They include *csirke paprikás*
(chicken paprika) and *gulyás* (goulash, a stew made from beef,
tomatoes, peppers, and carrots and flavored with chilli and
garlic). *Diós és mákos kalács* (walnut and poppy seed milk
bread) is a traditional Christmas dish.

the 18th century. The Hapsburgs, the ruling Austrian family, suppressed the Hungarian independence movement in 1849, and mass immigration to North America began. These immigrants became known as the "Forty-Niners." Many were members of the nobility and found it difficult to adjust to the American frontier. Nonetheless, few repatriated to Hungary.

The "Great Economic Migration"

The next wave of immigration, which took place in the three decades before World War I, comprised many of the poorest people from Hungary. In total, about 1.7 million Hungarian citizens, among them about 700,000 Magyars, arrived during what has been termed the "Great Economic Migration." These poor and uneducated immigrants came in search of new social and economic opportunities, but encountered prejudice in North America that persisted through both world wars. They remained in tight-knit communities and clung to Hungarian traditions not only because they wanted to, but because much of American society was hostile toward them.

Most of these immigrants hoped to collect enough capital to return to Hungary and buy land in order to become farmers. Few of them were able to gather sufficient funds, and only about 25 percent returned. Many of them were also dissuaded from returning by their American-born children, who wanted to distance themselves from their Hungarian roots and gain acceptance in American society. Still others had little desire to return to Hungary after it was divided up following World War I. At this time many former Hungarian lands were incorporated into the countries of Czechoslovakia, Yugoslavia, and Romania under the Treaty of Trianon (1920).

Immigration in the 20th Century

By the 1920s most of the Hungarian immigrants who arrived in the United States came to stay. They raised their families with the intention of integrating into U.S. society: that meant getting involved in the events of their local churches, societies, and cultural groups. Meanwhile, the start of World War I had ended mass migration to the United States. Immigration laws passed in 1921 and 1924 lowered the quota of Hungarian immigrants to 1,000 per year, and it remained valid until 1965. Despite these restrictions 600,000 Hungarians entered the United States under different classifications: refugee intellectuals in the 1930s, displaced persons following World War II, and "Fifty-Sixers," political refugees who left Hungary after the failed 1956 revolution. Among the

Béla Bartók

The Hungarian composer Béla Bartók was born in 1881 and began studying the piano with his mother while still a child. In addition to performing, Bartók composed music in the style of the day while often incorporating traditional Hungarian themes. He also transcribed traditional Hungarian folk music. In 1940 Bartók and his second wife reluctantly left war-torn Europe for America. Bartók died in New York in 1945.

Religion

In terms of religion Hungarian Americans are divided like Hungarian society. About 90 percent are Roman Catholics or Protestants (mainly Calvinists and Lutherans). The first Hungarian Reformed churches in America were established by Calvinists in Cleveland and Pittsburgh in 1891, followed in 1892 by the Roman Catholic church of Saint Elizabeth in Cleveland. By the 1930s Hungarian Americans had nearly 140 Calvinist churches, 60 Roman Catholic churches, and 10 Lutheran churches. Although there were fewer Roman Catholic places of worship, their congregations were much larger than those in Protestant churches.

A congregation worshiping in a Hungarian Reformed church in New York City in 1944.

Hungarian immigrants who came to North America the 1930s were leading nuclear physicists Edward Teller and Leo Szilard, who contributed to the development of science in the United States.

Traditions and the Relationship to the Homeland

Today the main issues for Hungarian Americans are the survival of their Hungarian traditions and their relationship to Hungary itself. Most Hungarian descendants are third, fourth, or fifth generation, and many do not speak the Hungarian language or consider themselves Hungarian. However, immigrants who arrived in the United States after World War II (1939–1945) have tended to foster their national heritage, and with their descendants many speak Hungarian at home.

Since the collapse of communism in the late 1980s and Hungary's independence in 1989–1990 a number of Hungarian Americans have repatriated to Hungary. Often Hungarian American employees of large western firms are sent to Hungary to set up branch offices, something that has helped renew ties with the homeland.

Recent Trends

Certain figures illustrate the decline in the Hungarian American population that has ties to its homeland. The number of people who identify themselves as Hungarian fell by 11 percent between 1980 and 1990 and a further 5 percent between 1990 and 2000, according to the U.S. census. In the 1980s alone, the number of families who primarily spoke Hungarian at home fell by about 18 percent. In the same decade Pittsburgh lost about half a dozen of its Hungarian churches, while numerous Hungarian organizations closed across Pennsylvania.

A notable characteristic of Hungarians in America is that they very rarely receive public assistance. Generally any form of welfare is seen as accepting a handout and is equated with failure. Hungarian family life is similar to that of Americans, but usually places a greater emphasis on education. Divorce among the Hungarian American community was significantly lower than the average American level until the 1990s. Now it has nearly reached average U.S. levels. Dating rituals in traditional Hungarian families are also stricter.

Holidays and Cultural Organizations

Hungarian Americans usually celebrate three major national holidays: March 15 (marking the 1848 Revolution), August 20 (St. Stephen's Day—Stephen was the first king of Hungary and is the nation's patron saint), and October 23 (marking the 1956 revolution).

Folk dancers in traditional dress performing at a festival in Hungary. The "Dance House Movement" of the 1970s revived folk music and dance in Hungary, and stimulated interest in these aspects of Hungarian culture in the United States and Canada.

Numerous groups, some of which were founded more than 50 years ago in North America, keep Hungarian folk dancing and folk culture alive. These aspects of Hungarian culture underwent a revival in the 1970s in Hungary. A movement called the "Dance House Movement" took the lead in this revival, responding to the anti-Hungarian cultural policy of the Soviet Union, which sought to weaken all things traditionally Hungarian. The influence of the "Dance House Movement" was felt in North America, where folk groups sprang up in many Hungarian communities.

Hungarian Americans have formed numerous community organizations in the United States. One of the first to be founded was the Hungarian Reformed Federation of America, established in 1896 in Trenton, New Jersey. It was originally intended to provide life insurance to Hungarians in America. Today its objectives are to "promote and strengthen the fraternal, spiritual, social, and cultural life of [its] people."

Organizing all of the Hungarian organizations in the United States is the Hungarian American Coalition. This umbrella organization works to identify and promote the aspirations, concerns, and interests of the Hungarian American community, and unites a wide range of other Hungarian-related groups, including religious organizations, political lobbies, local Hungarian clubs, and cultural groups.

Hungarian Americans have also set up organizations with the specific aim of helping Hungary. The most important are the Hungarian American Chamber of Commerce of New England, which works to promote investment in Hungary, and the Hungarian Human Rights Foundation, which campaigns to protect the rights of the Hungarian minority in Romania.

Hungary's success

Since the fall of communism in 1989 Hungary has been a leader in the economic changes that have taken place in eastern Europe. With its central location and its inexpensive and well-educated workforce, Hungary has been an ideal place for companies to set up European headquarters. Hungary has received over half of all foreign investments flowing to eastern Europe since 1990, and the country looks set for membership in the European Union, the economic union of Europe.

See also

- Austrians (Volume 1)
- Czechs (Volume 3)
- Romanians (Volume 9)
- Slovaks (Volume 9)

Hutterites

Hutterites specialize in farming crops and raising livestock, and in manufacturing goods both for colony use and for sale to outsiders. Male "bosses" assign and enforce work duties. A typical colony has a farm boss, a hog boss, a chicken boss, a cow boss, and so on for all of the jobs.

| Music |

Choral singing is an important part of the Hutterites' religious and social life. Church services include songs performed by choirs of young people, who also sing to the sick and the elderly and at important community events. Singing practice is usually held in the evening and provides an opportunity for choir members, who are often single, to socialize with each other and with young people from other colonies.

Children at the Forest River Hutterite colony in North Dakota say a prayer before breakfast. The people here live a communal life and share work on their 4,000–acre farm.

The Hutterites are a religious group. They are descendants of the Protestant Christian movement known as the Anabaptists and now live mainly in the western parts of the United States and Canada. They are distinctive for their very simple way of life, which is derived from their leaders' interpretations of the Bible and is centered around three religious beliefs. They believe in "communalism," or group sharing of all property; in "isolationism," or voluntarily living apart from mainstream society; and in "pacifism," or avoiding all acts of violence. Hutterites live together in communities called "colonies," each of which contains 60 to 130 people. Colony life consists of working, eating, and practicing religion together, although individual families live in separate houses. As of 2002 there were 42,000 Hutterites living in 428 colonies, making them the largest Christian communal group in North America.

Hutterite Beginnings

The earliest Hutterite group emerged in Central Europe in 1528 under the leadership of Jacob Huter. The Hutterites were originally German-speaking Anabaptists (those who practiced adult baptism) who believed that churches should be free from governmental control. They established a communal society in Moravia, but were harshly persecuted by other Christians in the area, and so they moved from place to place until finally settling in parts of Slovakia, Romania, Hungary, and the Ukraine. In the first 137 years of their existence the Hutterites' membership reached 25,000.

From 1874 until 1879 approximately 250 Hutterites from the Schmiedeleut, Dariusleut, and Lehreleut groups settled the southeastern region of South Dakota and later moved into other parts of the plains states. Many Hutterites moved to Canada in 1918 because they refused to fight in World War I and were persecuted by ultra-patriotic groups and the U.S. government. Today Hutterites live in colonies all over the western parts of North America, where they continue to follow the traditional ways of life that their ancestors established back in Europe.

Hutterite Heritage

Hutterites are known for their distinctively plain style of "old world" life. They wear practical clothes, like basic trousers and shirts for men and simple dresses for women. Male elders, including the minister and colony manager, make decisions for the community, while female elders are in charge of raising the families, educating the children in Hutterite kindergartens and schools, and preparing all the communal meals. As such, women have great influence on the life of the colony. All members of the community eat their meals together in a common building located at the center of the colony. Most important to Hutterite colonies, however, is religious worship. Hutterite life is centered around regularly scheduled daily church services. A minister leads the services, which are spoken in German, and his duties include conducting sermons, baptisms, marriages, and funerals.

Hutterites Today

Hutterites have been able to preserve many of their traditional customs, but that has created some challenges for the community. Their way of life is constantly threatened by pressures from the outside world. On the one hand, the Hutterites have adopted modern ways, like the use of gasoline-powered machinery and even computers. Yet they have also resisted ways of life that they believe would erode their faith and customs. They continue to speak German and to reject private property and service in the military. Few go to college, and fewer still marry someone from outside the colony. How future generations will respond to the challenges of the modern world is unclear. However, they do have low rates of divorce and crime, and this stability suggests that they will survive for many years to come.

Useful websites

Homepage for the Hutterian Bretheren (www.hutterites.org)
Hutterites: A Selected Bibliography (www.hutterites.info)
Hutterite Education (http://huttschools.freeyellow.com)
Riverview Hutterite Colony School (http://sesd.sk.ca/grassroots/Riverview)

See also

- Amish (Volume 1)
- Mennonites (Volume 7)
- Mormons (Volume 7)
- Religion (Volume 9)
- War and military service (Volume 10)

Fact File: HUTTERITES

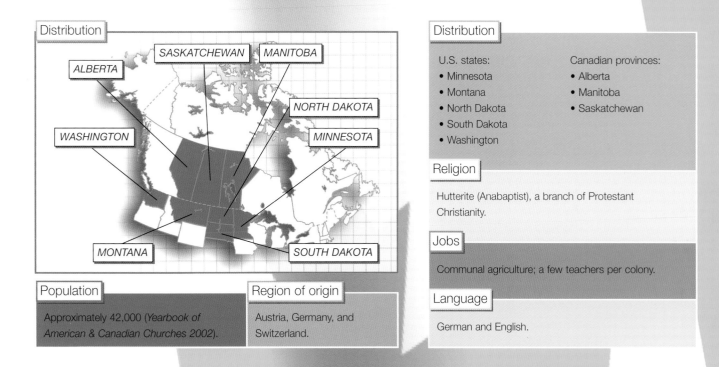

Distribution

U.S. states:
- Minnesota
- Montana
- North Dakota
- South Dakota
- Washington

Canadian provinces:
- Alberta
- Manitoba
- Saskatchewan

Religion

Hutterite (Anabaptist), a branch of Protestant Christianity.

Jobs

Communal agriculture; a few teachers per colony.

Population

Approximately 42,000 (*Yearbook of American & Canadian Churches 2002*).

Region of origin

Austria, Germany, and Switzerland.

Language

German and English.

Icelanders

Icelandic

The Icelandic language developed from Old Norse, the language of the Vikings, and has changed very little over the centuries. Not many Icelandic Americans speak Icelandic, but those who do can read medieval sagas—beautifully written accounts of Icelandic history and mythology—more easily than most English-speakers can read the works of Shakespeare.

See also

• Greenlanders (Volume 4)
• Literature (Volume 6)
• Norwegians (Volume 8)
• War brides (Volume 10)

Celtic monks and Norse Vikings settled the island of Iceland, which today is an independent republic. The first Icelandic immigrants to the United States were Mormon missionaries who moved to Utah in the 1850s. About 15,000 Icelanders (20 percent of the population) emigrated to North America between 1870 and 1900 to escape poverty and political unrest. Many settled on the prairies of Canada and in the north-central United States. Icelandic women also came to the United States as war brides after World War II (1939–1945).

Icelanders in North America

Icelandic immigrants learned English quickly and assimilated easily into North American culture. Most of them settled on farms, but financial hardship often forced the men to leave home and take jobs in commercial fisheries, railroads, and logging camps. Others started their own construction companies and other businesses. In general, the Icelandic community was highly literate and politically active. A strong literary tradition, stemming from the folklore of the heroic Norse sagas, led Icelandic Americans to achieve distinction as journalists, writers, and poets. Today, most Icelandic Canadians and Icelandic Americans are educated professionals living in large cities, and many of them take an active interest in their Icelandic heritage.

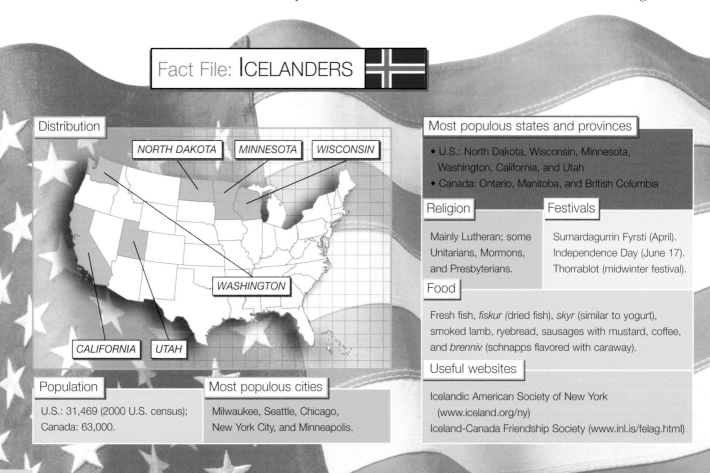

Fact File: ICELANDERS

Distribution

NORTH DAKOTA   MINNESOTA   WISCONSIN

WASHINGTON

CALIFORNIA   UTAH

Population

U.S.: 31,469 (2000 U.S. census);
Canada: 63,000.

Most populous cities

Milwaukee, Seattle, Chicago,
New York City, and Minneapolis.

Most populous states and provinces

• U.S.: North Dakota, Wisconsin, Minnesota, Washington, California, and Utah
• Canada: Ontario, Manitoba, and British Columbia

Religion

Mainly Lutheran; some Unitarians, Mormons, and Presbyterians.

Festivals

Sumardagurrin Fyrsti (April).
Independence Day (June 17).
Thorrablot (midwinter festival).

Food

Fresh fish, *fiskur* (dried fish), *skyr* (similar to yogurt), smoked lamb, ryebread, sausages with mustard, coffee, and *brenniv* (schnapps flavored with caraway).

Useful websites

Icelandic American Society of New York
(www.iceland.org/ny)
Iceland-Canada Friendship Society (www.inl.is/felag.html)

Illegal immigration

Immigrants are often considered to be at the core of America's strength and prosperity. The United States, composed of diverse immigrant peoples, prides itself on being a nation where opportunity and freedom abound. However, when immigrants enter the country without permission, the matter gets complicated. For example, it is very difficult to decide whether illegal immigrants should be given free healthcare, paid for by citizens' tax dollars, or whether their children deserve to be educated in government-funded public schools. Providing these services to illegal immigrants may strain public resources and be seen as unfair by taxpayers. Yet withholding healthcare and education from a part of the population raises serious moral questions and may create even greater problems for society in the longer term. Lawmakers constantly debate these matters, and the treatment of illegal immigrants and their children changes frequently.

Illegal Immigrants in the United States

A large percentage of illegal immigrants enter the United States for financial reasons. Most come from areas of the world that are less developed economically than the United States, and even low-skilled laborers are able to find higher-paying work in the United States than they could ever hope to find in their own countries. Though it is a crime for employers to hire illegal immigrants, they often do it anyway, because they save money by paying illegal workers less than the minimum wage they would be forced to pay documented laborers.

While legal immigrants currently constitute about 10 percent of the total U.S. population, illegals are thought to make up about 2 percent. Roughly 275,000 illegal immigrants enter the country each year, compared to one million who arrive legally, according to data from the U.S. Immigration and Naturalization Service (INS). INS border patrols catch and turn away a further one million people who are trying to enter the country without permission.

In the late 1980s and early 1990s about 2.7 million illegal immigrants residing in the United States were granted amnesty, or forgiveness, for their undocumented entry, as a result of the Immigration Reform and Control Act of 1986. However, the primary purpose of this law was to reduce the number of illegal aliens by making it more difficult for employers to hire workers without legal

Customs officers interview a man caught at the U.S. border with marijuana in his possession. Most illegal immigrants are not criminals, but are simply seeking a better life.

Tighter controls

The September 11, 2001, terrorist attacks, in which two hijacked airplanes were flown into the World Trade Center in New York (below), revealed how easily hostile foreign nationals could enter the United States. Thirteen of the Middle Eastern hijackers entered legally, mostly with student visas. As a result, the government has started monitoring foreign students. The other six hijackers apparently entered without proper documentation, prompting greater airline security and a reorganization of the INS. In June 2002 President Bush proposed a huge new cabinet agency called the Department of Homeland Security to oversee national security and immigration.

See also

- Anti-immigrant prejudice (Volume 1)
- Crossborder migration, Canadian (Volume 3)
- Immigration legislation (Volume 5)
- INS (Volume 5)

documentation. At the same time, the government took steps to improve border controls. Yet despite these new restrictions, the number of people who entered the country illegally soon climbed back to previous levels, according to government estimates.

Illegal Immigration over the U.S.–Mexico Border

Government patrols have been guarding the border between the country of Mexico and the U.S. states of California, Arizona, New Mexico, and Texas since the early 1900s. Inspectors first patrolled the border by horseback and later switched to motor vehicles. In the early days small teams of only a few officers guarded hundreds of miles in each state. Today there are more than 1,000 agents spread along the border, trying to catch an overwhelming number of trespassers.

Since the 1990s severe economic conditions in Mexico, as well as better law enforcement, have caused a substantial increase in drug smuggling and alien apprehensions, according to border patrol groups in New Mexico. Many political refugees from Central America also use the U.S.–Mexico border to cross into North America. However, most illegal immigrants cross the border to look for work or to be reunited with family members in the United States. They risk arrest and deportation by U.S. border patrol agents, and every year some are injured or even killed by extreme weather conditions and difficult terrain. Yet thousands of people successfully get past the patrols.

Once they cross the border, many illegal immigrants find work on farms in California or as dishwashers, gardeners, and nannies all across the Southwestern states and in several of the northern states. The INS estimates that more than 2 million illegal immigrants live in California today. In the entire United States an estimated 2.7 million out of 5 million illegal immigrants are Mexican.

Other Border Crossings

Illegal immigration across the Canada–U.S. border mostly involves foreigners from other countries. Before the terrorist attacks of September 11, 2001, the Canadian border was less strictly controlled than the Mexican border, because the number of illegal immigrants trying to enter the United States from Canada is far lower. However, in the aftermath of September 11 the United States and Canada agreed on new measures to tighten security along their shared border.

Immigrants to North America have always faced a variety of obstacles and challenges since people first began moving to the continent in the early 1600s. In recent years the establishment of government assistance programs and a gradual lessening of prejudices have all served immigrants well. Immigrants are still challenged, however, depending on how different their home countries and cultures are from the democratic, Western cultures of the United States and Canada. Race, language, cultural differences, and economic status play a role in how each immigrant assimilates, or becomes accustomed to a new culture. Most immigrants must cope with a certain amount of anxiety, loneliness, and family disruption.

Another fundamental challenge for immigrants is finding the right balance between native and adopted cultures. First-generation immigrants face the challenging task of preserving and passing on their culture and traditions to their children, who usually become Americanized quickly, while still helping them acquire the skills they will need to succeed in their new environment.

Early Immigrants

From the early 17th century Europeans of numerous nationalities flocked to North America in search of religious and political freedom, land to farm, and to exploit the continent's vast natural resources. Crossing the Atlantic by ship took between two and three months, and conditions were often harsh. Food shortages and cramped quarters increased the likelihood of disease, and many people died during the voyage. Once they landed, usually on the east coast of what later became the United States, they often faced starvation as a result of crop failures or became involved in clashes with Native American peoples that sometimes resulted in high casualty rates on both sides.

Africans and natives of the Caribbean began immigrating to North America against their will as slaves in the early 1600s. Torn from their homes and families, slaves endured great hardships, because their basic freedoms were denied and their living conditions were even more severe than those of their owners.

Life improved for many people as the British colonies on the eastern seaboard prospered. Thousands of immigrants pushed westward in the 1800s, working on the first transcontinental railroad, which linked the east and west coasts, and settling in new towns along the way.

Pearl Harbor

When the Japanese bombed Pearl Harbor on December 7, 1941 (below), the United States was immediately drawn into World War II (1939–1945), and racism erupted against Japanese Americans. In the eyes of the U.S. government all Japanese Americans became potential spies for their native country. As a result, 117,000 people of Japanese descent were herded into makeshift concentration camps in the Western states and interned for the duration of the war. Not one person taken into custody was found to be a spy, and the hurried act was later viewed as a serious violation of the internees' rights. When the war ended, Japanese Americans were freed but destitute, having lost their life savings, jobs, homes, and possessions. In 1988 the United States formally apologized to families of those interned and paid compensation of $20,000 to each internee. The move was widely criticized as too little, too late.

The move westward was an emotional journey as well as a physical one, especially for those who had escaped extreme hardship in their native countries. The Irish, for example, had fled a devastating famine caused by the destruction of the potato crop by disease in the 1840s, and many had been forced to leave sick or dying relatives behind.

Many immigrant groups in the 19th century were overwhelmingly male, especially those who worked on the railroads, creating an independent bachelor lifestyle. Minority immigrants, such as the Chinese laborers who were encouraged to come to the United States to help build the transcontinental railroad, usually lived and worked separately from others, creating their own communities.

Changing Attitudes toward Immigrants

The United States became a less welcoming place for immigrants in the 1860s, when new restrictions began to target the Chinese. In 1882 Congress passed the Chinese Exclusion Act, barring further Chinese laborers from entering the country. Between 1910 and 1940 the situation became even more restrictive. Angel Island in San Francisco Bay, California, was turned into a detention center for Chinese immigrants who were already present in the United States. Thousands of Chinese people were detained at the center, sometimes for years. Held in cramped, prisonlike rooms, some committed suicide or welcomed deportation back to their homeland.

Even though many U.S. and Canadian citizens were proud of their nation's immigrant heritage, citizens still discriminated against newcomers. Prejudice in the 1800s and early 1900s resulted in segregated communities, and immigrants had trouble gaining education and higher-paying jobs. Reports suggest that prejudice against foreigners and newcomers lessened when World War II ended in 1945, as people began to realize how destructive racial hatred could be. The racial policies of Adolf Hitler during the 1930s and the subsequent systematic murder by the Nazis of six million Jews provided one such tragic example.

Immigrants to North America today mainly settle in cities, where economic opportunities are usually more abundant. Depending on their background, immigrants can be found in a wide range of occupations. Some are university students, professionals, or own small businesses; while others do the jobs that U.S.-born workers do not want to do such as driving

Ten thousand immigrants from 73 countries are sworn in as U.S. citizens on June 22, 1981, in the largest such ceremony ever held.

cabs or working as farm laborers. Immigrants' experiences vary depending on how they arrived: whether legally or illegally, with or without money, with no connections or with a job and family members waiting. British, Irish, Scottish, and Australian immigrants tend to have the most in common with Americans and Canadians because of their shared language and (usually) white skin. These two factors make the transition much easier. For others, such as Asians and Eastern Europeans, a language gap or a "different" appearance can set back assimilation for years.

Recession and War

How well an immigrant is received by U.S. and Canadian citizens often depends on the state of the national or local economy. During recessions there has been a tendency to blame immigrants for taking the jobs of native-born workers. For example, during the 1930s many Mexican immigrants were forcibly repatriated from California and Texas on the grounds that they had a negative effect on the economy. While economists debate the validity of these claims, resentment against foreign-born workers remains a major political issue in the United States and Canada. However, the Canadian government has made the case that immigrants contribute to the country's economic growth, since Canada has a negative birthrate (the number of births in one year is fewer than the number of deaths).

The hardships suffered by Japanese immigrants during World War II, when more than 100,000 innocent Japanese Americans and 25,000 Japanese Canadians were rounded up and imprisoned because they were thought to be potential spies, have a parallel in the 21st century. In 2001 Middle Eastern immigrants became victims of heightened prejudice and suspicion when the U.S. "War on Terrorism," launched in the wake of the September 11, 2001, terrorist attacks, targeted some of their native countries. Many Middle Eastern business owners in the U.S. and Canada experienced a drop in sales or, worse, violence against them. In Chicago olive-skinned cab drivers—whether Middle Eastern or not—were harassed by customers and had to drive to the nearest police station for protection. The U.S. and Canadian governments condemn acts of harassment and violence, but immigrants continue to feel the effects of mistrust and fear.

Mexican workers pick strawberries in California. Many immigrants work hard at back-breaking jobs that few U.S.-born workers will do.

Teaching slang

English as a Second Language teachers sometimes incorporate American and Canadian slang words and phrases into their lesson plans. It is helpful even for English-speaking immigrants to know, for example, that "gross" means disgusting, a "high five" is when two people clap each other's hands in the air for congratulations, and "megabucks" is a lot of money.

設成玉砌變如籠
莫道其間皆西式
各位鄉君眾歡同
從今遠別此樓中

Detained in this wooden house for several tens of days.
It is all because of the Mexican exclusion law which implicates me.
It's a pity heroes have no way of exercising their prowess.
I can only await the word so that I can snap Zu's whip.

Economic Success and Hardship

Levels of immigration of certain groups depend on the employment needs of American companies. The demand for information technology (IT) workers has attracted many highly skilled workers from India. IT programming jobs in North America offer excellent salaries, and Asian Indian immigrants are one group that has prospered as a result. Recent U.S. Census reports show the median Asian Indian American family earning $60,093 per year, compared to the national median family income of $38,885. Asian Indian Americans are also known for their success as entrepreneurs, lawyers, doctors, engineers, and financiers.

The economic situation is drastically different for immigrants arriving with few professional skills, such as the many Mexican immigrants who cross the southwestern border of the United States. If an immigrant moves to the United States or Canada illegally, without a social security number and other documentation, it can be difficult to find legal employment or get a driver's license, and most undocumented workers end up working illegally for very low wages. Many illegal immigrants from Mexico work doubly hard to save money to buy their homes, since loans from a bank are also difficult or impossible to get in these cases.

Arriving as a refugee from faraway countries such as Iraq or Bosnia also puts up tremendous economic barriers. Having recently escaped treacherous circumstances in their home countries, most refugees have few financial resources, and many of them suffer the psychological effects of having been persecuted, intimidated, or physically harmed. Though assistance is available from the government, the first years in a new country are usually extremely hard for refugees. Steps toward financial stability and independence are made with the help of resettlement assistance organizations, such as church groups and government-run, nonprofit groups. American and Canadian volunteers assist in helping refugees find jobs, rent and furnish homes, and build up relationships within their new communities.

Learning English

The biggest challenge for non-English speaking immigrants is the language barrier. One such immigrant described her first experiences in the United States as a feeling of invisibility and deafness. For young immigrants the learning process is usually fairly rapid, but for older people it can be painfully slow. Language challenges are an ongoing concern for many immigrants, even after other basic needs—such as employment, housing, and general independence—are taken care of.

Useful websites

Ellis Island Immigration Museum (www.ellisisland.com)
Angel Island (www.angelisland.org)
Center for Immigration Studies (www.cis.org)
Lutheran Social Ministry of the Southwest: Refugee Resettlement Program (www.lsmsaz.com)

Being able to communicate with people outside their own households can help immigrants cope with the feelings of isolation that come from living in an unfamiliar culture. Though learning a new language is never easy, it is rewarding, and ultimately, mastering English can make an immigrant feel that he or she "really belongs."

Non-English-speaking immigrants typically enroll in English as a Second Language (ESL) classes, often taught at night by volunteers or local college instructors. The classes can be a good place for immigrants to meet sympathetic new friends who are struggling just as they are. Teachers focus not only on vocabulary and grammar, but also on useful conversation for specific situations, such as going shopping, asking for directions, or being interviewed for a job.

Traditions Lost and Found

A vast amount of culture and tradition is lost in the transition from immigrants' native countries to the United States and Canada. The concept of arranged marriages, for example, is common in many cultures such as India and Pakistan, but unheard of among Americans and is often abandoned by second-generation immigrants.

The Hmong population, one of the fastest-growing Asian-origin groups in the United States, is one example of an immigrant group that is deeply affected by its fading cultural identity. Originally from China, and more recently Southeast Asia, the Hmong suffered persecution by the government of Laos after the Vietnam War, in which the Hmong sided with the United States. As with many immigrant groups, there is a division in the Hmong between the

Sanjiv Sidhu

Many immigrants begin their new lives in the classroom and go on to great success. One extreme example is Sanjiv Sidhu of Hyderabad, India, who earned his master's degree in chemical engineering in the United States in 1982. Six years later, in Dallas, Texas, he founded software company i2 Technologies. Sidhu is now known as a pioneer in supply-chain software. In March 2001 Sidhu was named the wealthiest Indian immigrant in the United States by *Forbes ASAP* magazine, with a net worth of $6.8 billion. He ranked seventh out of 33 high-tech billionaires in another *Forbes* list. Indian immigrant Gururaj Deshpande, a cofounder of Sycamore Networks, also made the list, as did Pradeep Sindhu, founder of Juniper Networks.

Hmong sewing

The native art form of sewing is one example of a tradition that is fading away for the Hmong in North America. As a way of keeping their culture alive, these Hmong women from Syracuse, New York, have created a story cloth, or *pa ndau* (right), a hand-sewn quilt that illustrates the history of the Hmong people. Creating these intricate, colorful patterns on traditional clothing and blankets was once revered as a crucial skill for a Hmong woman, affecting both her self-esteem and her ability to attract a husband. Now, Americanized Hmong girls feel they do not have the time to learn to sew, and they can make more money from a minimum-wage job. Before, sewing was an issue of tradition, not profit.

original immigrants and the younger second generation. The young consider themselves very Americanized and have lives that are quite similar to those of their U.S.-born counterparts. Older Hmong men and women worry about the loss of their culture as their children and grandchildren move toward the American, capitalist way of life.

Russian immigrants are another example of an immigrant group that has moved in numbers to the United States since the 1960s and that has had to deal with issues of cultural identity. These Russians fled the economic hardship and political oppression of Soviet Russia. Russian Jews, in particular, migrated in numbers to the United States and Canada in the 1970s and 1980s. In Soviet Russia Judaism (the Jewish faith) had been outlawed, and consequently many Russian Jews had little idea of their cultural and religious heritage. Therefore, when Russian Jews moved to the United States, they often found it difficult to assimilate with the existing Jewish American communities that had a much stronger idea of their religious heritage.

Another recent immigrant group, immigrants from East Africa, has done its best to retain its cultures and customs in the United States by continuing to practice traditional skills, such as tailoring and hair braiding. In addition, East African community organizations work hard to preserve traditional practices by organizing weekend schools and camps where children of East African descent can learn about their parents' cultures and traditions.

The Immigration and Naturalization Service (INS) is an agency of the U.S. Department of Justice enforcing laws and providing services related to immigration and the naturalization of citizens. Overseen by a commissioner, and working in cooperation with a number of other government departments, the agency is operated by 29,000 employees with a total budget of $5 billion (in 2001). The INS works through four divisions: enforcement and examinations; field operations; policy and planning; and management services. The first two occupy the greatest number of staff and resources.

For purposes of administration the INS divides the United States into 33 geographic districts (including Alaska and Hawaii) and 21 Border Patrol sectors. To manage all its operations, the agency maintains three district offices: Burlington, Vermont (Eastern); Dallas, Texas (Central); and Laguna Niguel, California (Western). It also has 39 area offices outside the United States. The foreign offices assist with immigration visa applications and enhance the flow of immigration information between themselves and foreign governments.

The United States shares 6,000 miles (9,600km) of border with Mexico and Canada. The INS patrols these borders as well as overseeing 3,000 specific land, air, and sea ports of entry. In 2001 the agency conducted a total of 510 million inspections at its various ports and checkpoints. So large is its workload that the agency increased its staff by 79 percent between the years 1993 and 2001, mostly to implement inspections and to engage in other enforcement operations. It apprehended and deported a total of 176,549 criminal and other illegal aliens in 2001—the number of criminal cases alone exceeding the total number of all aliens deported in 1995. For the period between apprehension and deportation illegal aliens are held in nine INS detention facilities as well as in rented space in prisons and state and local jails. These centers are also used to hold detainees during their appeal processes.

The History of the INS

The structure and role of the INS have changed dramatically over time. The earliest office of the agency was established at the State Department in Washington, D.C., in 1864. Its main function was to encourage immigration and to offer protection to newcomers. However, since individual states had a great deal of latitude in making decisions on who could and could not immigrate, Congress decided to exert more federal

A married Haitian couple manage a few moments together in spite of the fence that separates their living quarters at the INS Krome Avenue North holding camp in Miami, Florida. The facility—a former missile base—is now used to detain illegal aliens prior to their deportation hearings.

A group of immigrants swear the American oath of citizenship at their naturalization ceremony.

The U.S. Oath of Allegiance

I hereby declare, an oath, that I absolutely and entirely renounce and abjure all allegiance and fidelity to any foreign prince, potentate, state or sovereignty, of whom or which I have heretofore been a subject or citizen; that I will support and defend the Constitution and laws of the United States of America against all enemies, foreign and domestic; that I will bear true faith and allegiance to the same; *that I will bear arms on behalf of the United States when required by the law; that I will perform non-combatant service in the armed forces of the United States when required by the law;** that I will perform work of national importance under civilian direction when required by law; and that I take this obligation freely without any mental reservation or purpose of evasion: So help me God.

*Under certain circumstances the italicized clauses are optional.

control. In 1891 it passed an Immigration Act that created a superintendent of immigration in the Department of the Treasury. It also established 24 inspection stations (one of which was Ellis Island in New York Harbor) to serve as legal points of entry to the United States.

Meanwhile, the U.S. government had to establish rules and regulations for determining who could become a naturalized citizen. When Congress passed the Naturalization Act in 1906, it solved this problem by outlining legal processes for citizenship. Immigration and naturalization functioned together for a few years until they were separated in 1913. The two were brought together once more under presidential Executive Order 6166 of June 10, 1933, issued by Franklin D. Roosevelt, to make them a single agency: The Immigration and Naturalization Service (INS). Over the next few years, as the agency became increasingly concerned with illegal immigration, the government moved the INS to the Department of Justice, which is where it has remained ever since.

The Quota System

The structures of the INS changed over time because people's reasons for wanting to come to the United States—and the reasons for the government admitting them—changed over time as well. At first it seemed to matter little how many people came or why, as long as they were white and were neither diseased nor poor. Soon, however, U.S. citizens began worrying that newcomers would be willing to work for less pay, which in turn would threaten their own jobs. This led to an act of Congress in 1921 that established quotas for U.S. admission according to country of origin. The quotas were determined as a percentage (initially 3 percent) of the number of people from that country already in the United States. Clearly, the law favored nationalities from northern European countries that already had a heavy representation in the population of the United States.

The quota system stayed in place for almost 60 years, but world events during this period influenced where the INS concentrated its resources. During the Great Depression of the late 1920s and 1930s, for example, the INS expanded its operations for exclusion and deportation, making it harder for outsiders to enter the country and become naturalized citizens, even for the thousands of European refugees fleeing Nazi persecution.

The INS faced a new era when thousands of people sought refuge in the United States from war-torn countries of both Eastern and Western Europe in the aftermath of World War II (1939–1945). President Harry S. Truman acted to allow 40,000 refugees to enter the United States without undergoing formal immigration and naturalization procedures. Later, provision was made for the temporary entry of anticommunist refugees from Hungary, Czechoslovakia, and Vietnam, under the immigration reforms of the 1960s.

It was not until the 1980s, when many more thousands sought refuge from conflict-riven Asian and Central American countries, that the INS became more aggressive in enforcing immigration statutes. The debate over asylum seekers and illegal immigrants gained momentum during the 1980s, when the volume of entrants increased dramatically, particularly from Mexico and Central America.

New Procedures

To respond to public pressure for greater border and immigration control, in 1991 the INS began to computerize its operations, established fingerprinting routines, and increased its border patrol capability. It more than doubled the number of detention bed spaces between 1995 and 2001 and sought to deport illegal aliens as quickly as possible. In 2001 the enforcement division of the INS spent five times more money on law enforcement procedures that it did on all other citizenship services.

After the terrorist assault on the World Trade Center in September 2001 the INS immediately came under the close scrutiny of the U.S. government and the American public. Emergency procedures were put into place (for example, provisions for student and tourist visas were tightened), while the government considered proposals to reorganize the INS once again. Later, in June 2002, President Bush announced plans for the Department of Homeland Security to protect the United States against terrorism. He told Americans that the department would "control our borders and prevent terrorists and explosives from entering our country." The objective of the department is to centralize the resources and operations of the existing government agencies that deal with security in a bid to make U.S. intelligence and law enforcement as efficient and effective as possible.

See also

- Anti-immigrant prejudice (Volume 1)
- Crossborder migration, Canadian (Volume 3)
- Crossborder migration, Mexican (Volume 3)
- Illegal immigration (Volume 5)
- Immigration legislation, U.S. (Volume 5)

An officer of the Immigration and Naturalization Service fingerprints a suspected illegal alien in Atlanta, Georgia. A new regime of improved procedures was introduced in 1991 to counter the growing numbers of illegal immigrants attempting to enter the United States.

In 1798 President John Adams was voted new executive powers to deport any foreigner he considered to pose a threat to the security of the United States. The Alien-Sedition Acts were enacted at a time of rising political tension between the United States and France.

The United States has always been a nation of immigrants—more than 60 million have come from countries worldwide since the first recorded influx in 1820—and so the country has a long history of passing, amending, repealing, and reconsidering laws that deal with immigrants. Sometimes these laws have been driven by the economy. When the economy is strong and jobs are plentiful, immigration is often made easier. Sometimes these laws have been driven by prejudice—fears that the ethnic makeup of the country was changing too rapidly and had to be slowed down. And sometimes the laws have been driven by politics, the fear that aliens may be potential threats to United States' security. However, until the terrorist attacks of September 11, 2001, and except for a period stretching from the post-World War I years of the 1920s through the Depression of the 1930s, World War II (1939–1945), and the early post-World War II years of the late 1940s, the United States had been an unusually welcoming country for foreigners.

Patterns of Immigration

In 2001 about 10 percent of the nation's 280 million people were foreign-born. In 1920, after a long period of huge migrations from Britain, Italy, Ireland, Germany, and elsewhere in Europe, some 14 percent of a population of 105 million were foreign-born. Generally these newcomers were admitted with the blessing of the government, but nonetheless, some immigration legislation passed by Congress has been distinctly unfriendly. The first important immigration laws were enacted in 1798. Known as the Alien-Sedition Acts (alien meaning "foreigner"), they were passed during an antialien wave inspired by tense relations with France. About 25,000 French-born people lived in the United States at the time, and there was great fear that they would act against the United States in case of a confrontation between the two nations. The new Alien Act, passed for two years only, authorized President John Adams to deport any foreigner he deemed "dangerous to the peace and safety of the United States." In addition the Sedition Act made it illegal for anyone to speak or write against the president or Congress.

A Nation of Immigrants

Also in 1798 Congress adopted a Naturalization Act that required aliens to reside in the United States for 14 years before becoming eligible for citizenship. In 1802 this requirement was changed to five years. From this time until very near the end of the 19th century the

United States was open to immigrants with virtually no exceptions. Indeed, some legislation openly encouraged immigration to help populate and provide labor for the rapidly expanding nation. In 1819, for instance, Congress passed the Steerage Acts, setting health standards for passenger ships arriving in the United States. The law also required ship captains to provide passenger lists, which served as the country's first formal immigration records. Those lists tell the story of how open the United States was—and how appealing it was for so many. In the 1830s, 600,000 immigrants settled in the United States; in the 1840s, 1.7 million; the 1850s, 2.5 million; the 1860s (which included the four years of the Civil War), 2.3 million; the 1870s, 2.8 million; the 1880s, 5.2 million; and the 1890s, 3.6 million.

Until 1860 the vast majority of immigrants came from three countries: Ireland, Germany, and Great Britain. Huge numbers of Irish started arriving in the 1840s during the great potato famine in Ireland. So, while 207,000 Irish came during the 1830s, ships swelled with 780,000 Irish during the 1840s and 914,000 in the 1850s. As more and more Irish arrived, an intense anti-Irish feeling grew in the United States, and many Irish were discriminated against. A German economic crisis in the 1840s stimulated a similar rush to the United States. Only 152,000 Germans came in the 1830s, but that number rose to 434,000 in the 1840s, 951,000 in the 1850s, and 787,000 in the 1860s. It jumped again to 1.4 million in the 1880s. Immigration from Britain peaked in the 1880s at more than 807,000. After 1860 larger numbers arrived from Russia and Scandinavia, and the flow of Italians and Polish and others from eastern and southern Europe also grew. This vast pool of humanity, much of it not well educated, was a perfect source of labor for America's burgeoning industrial economy, but these new immigrants were different from the earlier immigrants and, like the Irish before them, were feared and resented by many Americans.

Restrictions on Immigration

Attitudes to open immigration began to change in 1882, with the first important immigration laws in nearly 100 years—laws that for the first time restricted immigrant numbers. Some 789,000 immigrants had arrived in the United States in that year, a number that would not be equaled until 1904. One of the acts of 1882 Congress, reacting to concerns about the cost of supporting immigrants unable to fend for themselves, blocked entry for "lunatics," "idiots," and others who needed to be cared for, as well as most convicts. Exceptions were made

A political cartoon of 1882 at the time of the Chinese Exclusion Act. It depicts a Chinese man clinging to freedom while being assailed by Irish workers (represented by a tiger) and the Republican Party (shown here as an elephant). The act suspended the immigration of Chinese laborers for 10 years.

Doctors examine a group of immigrants at the Ellis Island reception center in 1943. Medical examinations were first introduced in the late 19th century to ensure that the immigrant intake was disease-free.

for those convicted of political offenses. In 1891 Congress widened the list of unacceptable immigration applicants by adding polygamists and "persons suffering from a loathsome or a dangerous disease."

In the second major act of 1882—the Chinese Exclusion Act—Congress suspended the immigration of Chinese laborers for 10 years. The act was extended indefinitely in 1892 and not repealed totally until 1952. The act was the first ever to limit entry on the basis of race or ethnicity. More restrictive legislation was to come. In 1906, for the first time, aliens had to speak some English in order to become a citizen. In 1907 came the so-called "Gentleman's Agreement" with Japan under which the United States agreed not to ban Japanese immigration, and the Japanese agreed not to issue passports for laborers. Thus, except for some agricultural workers who were permitted to enter Hawaii, only Japanese businessmen and professionals were welcome. The 1917 Literacy Test, on which aliens had to prove they could read, was also designed to discourage non-English speaking immigrants.

Nevertheless, some 27 million immigrants arrived in the United States between 1860 and 1920, when several factors combined to end the liberal era of immigration and start a new era of quotas (the setting of specific limits on the number of immigrants who could enter the United States from each country of the world). Those factors included World War I (1914–1918), when there was a backlash against German Americans, and unemployment, which started to grow after the war had ended. Many Americans worried that immigrants were taking their jobs because they would work for less money. Fears about foreign radicals coming to stir up revolution against the government grew during the war and particularly after the 1917 communist revolution in Russia. Bigotry also inspired a negative reaction against the new immigrants from southern and eastern Europe, who looked different and had different habits than most Americans. In 1921 came

Political radicals awaiting deportation on Ellis Island in 1920. Following the communist revolution in Russia in 1917, there were widespread fears that anarchists and radicals would attempt to foment civil strife in the United States.

the first law to set quotas on immigration: Admissions from any European country would be limited to 3 percent of the population from that country who were already living in the United States in 1910. This formula was favorable to people from northwestern Europe because many more of them were in the United States in 1910.

The Quota System

Three years later the quota system became stricter, and it remained strict for decades. The 1924 law was known as the Johnson–Reed Act, and it had an immediate effect. Under this law admission from any country was reduced to 2 percent of the population from that country then living in the United States. The base year for calculating the exact number to be permitted entry was pushed back from 1910 to 1890, meaning that far fewer refugees could be admitted, and an even larger percentage would come from northwestern Europe (by 1890 few southern and eastern Europeans had arrived). The goal, said one Congressional report, was to keep "the basic strain of our population." The results were stark: In 1924, 706,000 immigrants entered the United States legally; in 1925 the number was 294,000. As a result, the number of illegal immigrants increased. During the 1930s—the period of the Great Depression and the beginning of World War II—the number of legal immigrants fell to fewer than 100,000 a year, the lowest numbers since the 1830s. The 1924 law was not completely revoked until 1965.

Immigration after World War II (1939–1945)

In 1940 laws were passed making it easier to deport aliens thought to be communists. In 1948 Congress passed the humanitarian Displaced Persons Act to accept people from countries destroyed in World War II. Ultimately, 390,000 people were admitted under the law. Laws passed in 1950, when the power of the communist Soviet Union was growing, allowed the U.S. government to deport noncitizens who belonged to the Communist Party or who might engage in "subversive" activities. The McCarran–Walter Act of 1952 made it easier for some nationalities, such as the Chinese, to enter the United States, but it favored people who had something to contribute to the culture or

Ellis Island

Ellis Island, near the tip of Manhattan, New York, was opened in 1892 as the main receiving center for European immigrants. Ultimately, 12 million people had their medical and legal examinations there before passing into the United States. The busiest years, though, ended in the early 1920s, when Congress enacted new legislation making it harder for immigrants to enter the United States. Ellis Island closed in 1954 and is now an immigration museum where visitors can search the records for their ancestors.

economy of the United States and was primarily directed against European immigrants suspected of "leftist" political views. In addition, the McCarran–Walter Act stipulated—for the first time in American legal history—that those people wishing to become U.S. citizens had to be able to read and write English as well as speak it.

Finally, in 1965, with racial prejudice beginning to decline, the quota system was changed. A maximum of 170,000 immigrants a year would now be accepted from the Eastern Hemisphere, with a maximum of 20,000 from any single country. Priority was given to family members of U.S. citizens and long-term residents. Similar rules were put in place for the Western Hemisphere in 1968. One exception to these provisions was Cuba. After Fidel Castro's communist revolution in 1959 the United States accepted all Cubans seeking to enter.

President Ronald Reagan signs a landmark immigration reform bill at the White House on November 6, 1986. The bill gave certain illegal aliens a chance at citizenship and included sanctions against employers who employed undocumented workers.

Recent Legislation

Over the next 20 years entrance to the United States became a goal for millions of illegal immigrants, many from Central and South America. Mexicans, particularly, would cross the U.S. border and try to find the low-paid work that Americans shunned, mostly in agriculture and factories. With so many "illegals" in the United States, in 1986 the U.S. Congress passed the Immigration Reform and Control Act and gave amnesty to around three million illegal residents. Anyone who had been living in the United States since before 1982 could get permanent legal status. However, to discourage the arrival of more illegal aliens, the new law punished employers who hired them. Illegal immigration did not stop as a result, and so in 1996 Congress passed legislation making it easier to deport residents and more difficult for undocumented aliens to acquire legal status in the United States.

Fresh concerns were raised over immigration laws by the events of September 11, 2001, when 19 Islamic terrorists killed 3,000 people when they hijacked four commercial planes and crashed two of them into the World Trade Center in New York City and one into the Pentagon, near Washington, D.C. Measures were taken to tighten the security on the U.S.–Canada border, and the Department of Immigration and Naturalization was restructured to become part of a unified border security and domestic defense department.

See also

- Anti-immigrant prejudice (Volume 1)
- Assimilation (Volume 1)
- Canadian immigration/emigration (Volume 2)
- Cultural mingling (Volume 3)
- Illegal immigration (Volume 5)
- Immigrant experience (Volume 5)
- Immigration and Naturalization Service (Volume 5)
- Mexican immigration/emigration (Volume 7)

Indonesians

The Republic of Indonesia in southeast Asia consists of 17,508 islands that are home to a population comprising more than 300 ethnic groups. The largest ethnic group are the Javanese. They come from Java, the fourth largest island in the republic, and account for about half the population of Indonesia. In 1993 the population of Indonesia was 191 million people, making it the fourth most populous country in the world. Very few Indonesians immigrated to North America before 1950, when Indonesia gained independence from over 300 years of Dutch rule.

Recent Immigrants

Indonesians have not traditionally immigrated to North America. Many of the Indonesians currently in North America are recent arrivals—85 percent of them are foreign-born—and most are from the larger cities on Java. The relatively small population of Indonesian immigrants in 2000 (39,757) is four times the size it was in 1980 (9,618). Due to these small numbers, and the great religious and racial diversity among Indonesians, no identifiable Indonesian American communities exist in North America. Instead, most Indonesians choose to settle in already established Asian American communities.

Higher Education

The most recent Indonesian Americans have come to North America to seek higher education in colleges and graduate schools. Many study engineering or the social sciences. Their education level is very high compared to the general population of Indonesia. As a result, nearly

Notable Indonesian Americans

Joyce Kennard, associate justice of
California Supreme Court.
Jahja Ling, conductor and pianist.
Fatimah Tobing Rony, filmmaker,
film scholar, and professor of
Asian American studies.

Gamelan orchestras

Perhaps the most defining music of Indonesia is the gamelan. Thousands of years old, gamelan orchestras (left) feature percussion instruments with up to 80 different sizes of gongs, chimes, cymbals, wood xylophones, and drums. Flutes, stringed instruments, and vocalists accompany and "answer" the percussion instruments. The different islands and regions of Indonesia each feature their own variation of gamelan instruments and traditions. The Javanese traditionally used the soothing yet intricate gamelan sounds as court music. The Balinese considered it music for the gods. Today, many universities in North America feature performing gamelan ensembles.

Batik cloth

The word batik comes from the Javanese *tik*, and means "to dot." Indonesians wear sarongs made of batik cloth as their traditional dress. To make batik, an artist uses an apparatus called a *tjanting* to draw intricate designs in hot wax onto cotton cloth. When the cloth is dyed, the part covered with wax resists the color. The artist removes the wax and repeats the process with different colors. Batik is an important export of Indonesia.

See also

• Singaporeans (Volume 9)
• Thais (Volume 10)
• Vietnamese (Volume 10)

one-quarter of the current population of Indonesian Americans are between the ages of 25 and 34, and a majority of them are male. A majority are also single; but since Indonesians are usually quite family oriented, this undoubtedly reflects their student status and youth.

In the 1990s the Indonesian economy grew rapidly, and President Clinton's 1994 visit to an economic summit in Jakarta spurred trade with North America. Many Indonesian Americans found work in the export and import industries. However, in 1998 the Indonesian economy spiraled out of control and threatened to collapse. Political instability followed, and the Indonesian people, led by student protesters, forced President Suharto from power after his 30-year reign. Political upheaval continued the next year in East Timor, where there was bloody protest against the province's upcoming vote for independence. This political and economic chaos led to an increase in the numbers of people wanting to emigrate.

Meanwhile, Indonesian Americans divide their loyalty and interest between North America and the Indonesian province where they or their family once lived. They continue to follow current events in Indonesia through print publications such as the *Indonesian Journal* and *Indonesia Letter* and websites that link to Indonesian newspapers.

Fact File: INDONESIANS

Distribution

NEW YORK | New York City
CALIFORNIA
Chicago
ILLINOIS
San Francisco | Los Angeles | TEXAS | Houston

Most populous states and cities

• States: California, Texas, New York, Illinois.
• Cities: Los Angeles, San Francisco, Houston, New York, and Chicago.

Population

U.S.: 39,757 (2000 census)

Dates of major arrivals

• 1953–1962: Indo-Europeans (of Dutch and Indonesian heritage) arrived.
• Late 1950s: Indonesians seeking higher education.
• Post-1968: Chinese Indonesians arrived.
• Post-1998: Following President Suharto's demise.

Jobs

Managers, professionals, and technical, sales, and administrative support.

Names

Chandra, Lie, Halim, Iskandar, Budiman, Sari, Suryana.

Community organizations

• American Indonesian Chamber of Commerce (www.aiccusa.org)
• Dharma Wanita (Indonesian American Society) has chapters in several U.S. states

The founders and early settlers of the United States of America were mainly from England, but many were also from Holland, Germany, France, and other European countries. Prior to 1800 immigrants did not arrive in large waves. Most were not employees as we know them today but farmers, slaves, or skilled tradesmen practicing the professions of their European ancestors. The first wave of mass immigration began in the early 1800s. Most of those immigrants were agricultural workers.

Manufacturing Industry

Between 1820 and 1860 industry grew in the northern United States. Factories produced labor-saving farm machinery, the telegraph improved communications, and railroads provided more efficient transportation of goods. As the economy expanded, factories produced more goods, and technology made goods cheaper. Craft workers became laborers, and old trades such as shoemaking and tailoring faded away. North American mills and factories sent representatives overseas to find skilled workers in countries such as Great Britain. Textile mills employed hand-loom weavers from England and Northern Ireland whose jobs had been displaced by power looms, helping to establish the fine-cotton-goods trade of Philadelphia. New England mills recruited women from Scotland who were expert weavers of gingham (a fabric with a design of alternate white and colored squares).

During this period five million immigrants arrived in the United States, more than the entire 1790 population. Four million arrived in the 1840s and 1850s alone. Many came with the expectation that they would make enough money to improve their economic situation and return home to Europe. Immigrants became an integral part of the northern economy, providing cheap labor for industry. The two most significant groups were the Irish and Germans. Their immigration was largely concentrated in the Northeast and the Midwest.

Between 1845 and 1860, 1.5 million Irish arrived in the United States. Disease had destroyed potato crops across Europe, causing famine, especially in Ireland. Desperately poor and unable to buy land, Irish immigrants crowded into poor neighborhoods in the cities where the ships docked. They provided industrial labor and the labor for canals, railroads, and other infrastructure projects that crisscrossed the nation.

In the 1850s one million German immigrants arrived in the United States, fleeing after unsuccessful revolutions in Germany. They were

Immigrants being enlisted in the U.S. Army outside Castle Garden, the Commission of Emigration building in New York City, in 1864. Duties and pay rates are advertised on the noticeboard at left, above which a small band plays military music.

Transatlantic labor market

During the early 20th century a lucrative and mutually beneficial transatlantic labor market developed in Canada and Europe in a bid to populate the west of the new country. Canada's Immigration Department paid North Atlantic Trading Company booking agents a $2 bonus for every "suitable" immigrant they sent to Canada. These immigrants included farmers, gardeners, domestics, laborers, and miners. Between 1906 and 1914 immigration from Britain to Canada increased from 86,800 to 142,600.

Workers harvesting tobacco by hand in North Carolina. Tobacco was an important crop from early colonial times and remains a significant source of employment today.

African Americans

African American immigrants who achieved notable success in industry and business included:

Macon Allen, the first African American licensed to practice law (1845).

Henry Blair, the inventor of corn and cotton seed planters.

Henry Boyd, the proprietor of a large furniture company.

Norbert Rillieux, the inventor of a machine that revolutionized the way sugar was made.

John Russworm, editor of *Freedom's Journal*, the first African American newspaper.

William Whipper, the owner of a lumber yard in Pennsylvania who devoted time and money to ending slavery.

African American workers check the weight of a bale of cotton on a Mississippi plantation in 1950. Cotton has always been the most important cash crop of the South.

from many German regions and included many German Jews. They also came for economic reasons, but were generally more skilled and wealthier than the Irish. Many Germans worked in northern factories and saved money to move west and buy farmland. Others worked as tailors, artisans, and merchants, including grocers and bakers.

Whether they were recruited directly for their abilities or found unskilled jobs through their own networks, immigrants tended to move within groups of friends and relatives and work and live in clusters. Cities grew rapidly. Chicago—which had 12 families in 1831, 30,000 people in 1850, and 1.7 million people in 1900—became the center of the meat-processing and packing industry.

The Civil War gave the United States a final push into the industrial age. A second wave of mass immigration followed significant growth in manufacturing in the period between 1861 and 1890. Western European immigrants entered industries on the East Coast, and Chinese immigrants joined the labor force in California. Immigration from China was outlawed in 1882, however, and remained illegal until 1943, when 105 Chinese immigrants were admitted. Not until 1965 was the limit on Chinese immigration significantly raised.

Industry in the South

In the southern United States the invention of the cotton gin in 1793 dramatically decreased the time needed to clean cotton; one slave could do the work of 1,000 using the cotton gin. However, as cotton became profitable, more slaves were needed to work in the fields, and the demand for slaves increased. Cotton became the country's largest cash crop; tobacco, rice, and sugar cane were also very important. However, the South remained dependent on the northern industrial centers and on Europe for a variety of finished goods.

By 1860 slaves made up one-third of the population of the South. Most worked as field hands on cotton plantations. Some became skilled workers such as carpenters and blacksmiths. Very few lived as if they were free; their earnings belonged to their owners. Of more than four million African Americans, only 200,000 were free in 1860; most were slaves. By the 1880s thousands of freed African Americans lived in the North, where they continued to be denied equal rights, faced discrimination, and had trouble finding good jobs.

The American West

The frontier between the settled lands of the East and the wild lands of the West was pushed farther and farther westward in two waves as land was bought, explored, and taken over by the United States government and settled by immigrants from Europe. Encouraged to move west by the Homestead Act of 1862, which offered public land free to immigrants who intended to become citizens, Germans comprised a large portion of the pioneers moving west.

After the Louisiana Purchase of 1803 a first wave of pioneers settled land as far west as the Mississippi River valley. The rich natural resources of the Midwest—Illinois, Iowa, Michigan, Ohio, Wisconsin, and Minnesot—attracted farmers, miners, and lumbermen. The second wave settled lands west of the Mississippi to California. Farms, ranches, and mines sprang up. The Chinese immigrant population in particular worked on the building of the railroads in the 1850s, and the California Gold Rush of 1848 and 1849 saw many other groups move west. Many of these immigrants suffered or died in the deserts, or due to Indian raids or outlaw violence.

The Great Plains in the center of the United States are made up of high plains to the west and low plains to the east. Many immigrants known as "sodbusters" (the initial settlers of the low plains who turned lush prairies into plowed fields) were of German and Scandinavian origin. On the high plains low rainfall made farming unprofitable; but the land was suitable for livestock, and cattle and sheep ranches were soon plentiful. One job in particular—the role of the cowboy—summed up most people's ideas of the West as a place of freedom and adventure.

Immigrant Employment Today

Immigrant groups, especially those with few skills and only a basic command of English, often have to adapt and take any work that is available. The tendency for companies to seek cheap labor that started in the 19th century continues today. In recent years the fastest-growing immigrant group to the United States has been from Latin America, many of whom have had to accept unskilled, low-paid work as their only form of employment.

German entrepreneurs

Bavarian immigrant Levi Strauss planned to make tents for miners in the 1849 gold rush in California, but ended up making trousers out of a tough fabric called *serge de Nîmes* (denim). We know them today simply as "jeans." German Jewish Americans such as Jacob and Isaac Gimbel and Joseph and Lyman Bloomingdale became department store magnates. John Stetson, in Philadelphia, created the first Stetson hat for miners, calling it "the Boss of the Plains."

Packers at work in a Chicago meat-processing plant in 1937. The meat industry was and remains a major employer for the city.

See also

- Agriculture (Volume 1)
- Labor unions (Volume 6)
- Stores and storekeepers (Volume 10)
- Trades and professions (Volume 10)

Intermarriage

Intermarriage is the name given to a marriage of two people from different ethnic, religious, or racial groups. When people from different ethnic groups marry, such as Americans and Germans, that is called an "intercultural marriage." Another type of intermarriage, called an "interfaith marriage," is when the most fundamental difference between spouses is religious preference. An example of an "interfaith" marriage would be a person of Jewish faith marrying one of Catholic faith. "Interracial" marriage, a third type, is between people who are from the same culture, but not the same genetic heritage. An example of interracial marriage would be an Asian American marrying an African American. The different types of intermarriage are all common in the United States and Canada. In practice, one marriage could qualify as one, two, or three types of intermarriage. For example, a Protestant African American marrying a Jewish Israeli would be a combination of all three types of intermarriage.

Early History of Intermarriage

During the colonial period of North America Native Americans were forced to adapt to new conditions. Although there was some inter-marriage between white settlers and Native Americans, it was nearly always between white men and Native American women. In particular, there was interaction between the "Five Civilized Tribes" (Cherokee, Chickasaw, Chocktaw, Creek, and Seminole) and the new white settlers in America. In Canada, too, there was intermarriage between the Native Americans and European settlers, the children of whom became known as the Metis, meaning "mixed blood."

In 1954 John Hewitt lost his teaching job at a school in Canada because of his interracial marriage to his wife Dorothy. Today the majority of Canadians have abandoned such racial prejudices.

However, Native Americans were generally not accepted in new white communities. Many indigenous peoples were put on reservations, and their land was taken from them. Often children were separated from their parents and placed in residential schools. This treatment of Native Americans established a pattern of behavior by whites toward nonwhites that was to continue until the 21st century.

There have never been laws restricting interreligious marriages in the United States. However, from the 17th century until the middle of the 20th century there were many legal barriers to interracial marriages, especially in the South and Southwest. Even until 1967, 19 states—17 of them in the South—had antimiscegenation laws (laws that prohibited marriage of whites to members of another race). There were also strong social barriers against the mixing of races. African Americans were subject to extreme racial discrimination in parts of the South. From 1882 until 1930 an estimated 2,500 blacks were lynched in the Southern states by white mobs, and blacks continued to face racial animosity in the first half of the 20th century from white supremacist organizations such as the Klu Klux Klan. In California state legislation prohibited intermarriage between whites and Chinese, Japanese, Filipinos, and other nonwhites until the 1960s.

Intermarriage and Immigration

Despite the many barriers against intermarriage, extensive immigration to North America has made it possible for a large number of ethnic, religious, and racial groups to interact. Today in the United States and Canada there are many factors that affect levels of intermarriage—differences in economic position, differences in the ability to speak English, the number of suitable partners, and social barriers. If an ethnic group is poor, its members are more likely to marry members of ethnic groups that are more prosperous or that give them higher status within society. Another major consideration is the number and availability of suitable partners in a person's own ethnic group. If a large number of potential partners is available, intermarriage with other ethnic groups is less likely. Also, many ethnic groups remain distinct from mainstream society in North America because of language differences. The adoption of English increases contact with people outside the group and makes ethnic intermarriage more likely. Finally, the barriers imposed by a group on intermarriage vary from group to group. The acceptance of a spouse from outside the ethnic, religious, or racial group often varies from family to family, place to place, and time to time, based on the individuals involved.

In this 1871 cartoon a mother and father are horrified that their son has married a black woman. Many people in the 19th century feared "miscegenation," or mixing of races.

The 1967 movie *Guess Who's Coming to Dinner?* was one of Hollywood's first attempts to address the issue of racial intermarriage. A young white woman (Katharine Houghton) returns home with her black fiancé (Sidney Poitier). Both sets of parents are shocked that their children plan to marry someone of a different race, but they sit down to dinner to try to resolve their differences. Acceptance of black–white marriages has been growing since the 1960s.

Intercultural Marriage

Historically, intercultural marriage was rare due to geographic isolation, language differences, and lack of contact with outsiders. Since ethnic groups share a common heredity, language, religion, geographic location, and behavior, marriage within the group preserves the group's ethnic distinctiveness.

The 1969 National Population Survey gives a picture of the rates of intercultural marriage among Americans at the time. The husbands were asked to give their ethnic origin, then asked if their wives were of the same group or a different group. Among European respondents the husbands who had wives from a different ethnic group were English (55 percent), German (66 percent), Irish (68 percent), Italian (47 percent), Polish (59 percent), and Russian (53 percent). Several sources report that intercultural marriage has consistently increased since 1971, both for immigrants and for native-born Americans, suggesting that the rate of intercultural marriage is even higher among these groups today.

One of the most distinctive side effects of intercultural marriage in the United States is the decrease in people who want to or are able to identify themselves with a single ethnic group. The 1969 National Population Survey reported that 50 percent of Americans either did not want to or could not identify their ethnic heritage.

Interfaith Marriage

In some ways interfaith marriages are the most challenging. A couple may forget about their racial differences or enjoy celebrating each other's cultural heritage, but it may be harder to maintain separate faiths for personal and social reasons. Some religious groups require outsiders to be formally converted to their religion before they are allowed to marry into the group. Even for marriages in which neither partner undergoes formal conversion, many interfaith marriages tend to become same-faith marriages over time. One study in Detroit, Michigan, showed that of 91 interfaith couples, 52 later began to follow the same faith.

Statistics are not available in the United States for interfaith marriages because the Census Bureau has been forbidden by law from keeping such records. The only year for which a nationwide survey of intermarriages is available is 1957. An analysis of this data shows that 12.1 percent of Catholics, 4.5 percent of Protestants, and

Ethnic groups respond in different ways to crosscultural dating. Some religious groups, such as the Mennonites and Mormons, believe that dating an outsider is a serious problem and should be strongly discouraged. Among other groups many people date and marry outside the group without difficulty.

3.7 percent of Jews had spouses from another religious group. It is likely that the statistics are somewhat low, based on the fact that a significant number of people change from their childhood religion to the religion of their spouse before marriage. These statistics only include people who claimed different religions at the time of marriage, and not those who may have converted beforehand.

Canada has in the past provided some information about the religion of the bride and groom at the time of marriage, although the government does not currently collect such data. Canadian statistics from the mid-20th century show a marked increase in the number of interfaith marriages. In 1927, 5 percent of Protestants, 7.2 percent of Catholics, and 3 percent of Jews were married outside their faith. By 1972 these numbers had risen substantially, and 22.7 percent of Protestants, 20.5 percent of Catholics, and 15.4 percent of Jews were married to someone of a different faith.

Interracial Marriage

The term "interracial" tends to be hard to define because the term "race" can be ambiguous. Interracial marriage usually refers to the lineage of physically distinct groups, such as blacks, Native Americans, Asians, Hispanics, whites, or mixed lineages. The topic is further complicated by the fact that data on interracial marriage varies because different states use different definitions. Today the U.S. Census allows a self-definition of race, which says that "You are of that race if you think you are." For example, there are many groups that could be classified as white but are not of European descent, such as Mexicans and Arabs. According to the government, they are white if they consider themselves to be white.

Intermarriages among all racial groups are increasing, although it is thought that marriage between blacks and whites is less common than intermarriage among other nonwhite racial groups. In 1992 interracial marriages between blacks and whites accounted for less than 1 percent of all U.S. marriages, and according to the 1994 National Health and Social Living Survey, 97 percent of black women in the United States are likely to chose a partner of the same race.

However, as with intercultural marriages, there has been a dramatic rise in the social acceptance of interracial marriages. For example, in 1968, 52 percent of Canadians disapproved of black–white marriages; in 1995 the approval rating was 81 percent. It is likely that given time, a large proportion of all intercultural, interfaith, and interracial marriages will enjoy the same wide acceptance.

Zubin Mehta with his wife, Nancy. At the time of their marriage in 1969 Nancy Kovack was a well-known Hollywood actress. Zubin Mehta, who immigrated from his native India, was then the director of the Los Angeles Philharmonic. Today intermarriages like this one are common in the United States and Canada.

See also

- Assimilation (Volume 1)
- Cultural mingling (Volume 3)
- Multiple ethnic origins (Volume 7)
- Social mobility and race (Volume 9)
- War brides (Volume 10)

Inuit

One of the most distinctive aspects of the traditional Inuit lifestyle was a reliance on sled dogs. The Canadian Inuit dog, as the breed is now known, has probably existed for about 4,000 years. It was bred to pull heavy loads and cope with extreme cold. Teams of dogs hauled game and moved Inuit families and their possessions from place to place. A special harness let the dogs fan out instead of following each other in a line, so it was safer for them to cross thin ice. Lifestyle changes among the Inuit have led to a decline in the everyday use of sled dogs, but dogsledding is gaining popularity as a sport, and there is renewed interest in many northern breeds. In recognition of the Canadian Inuit dog's cultural significance, the Nunavut Territory has chosen it as the official "state" animal.

An Inuit elder sits by the shore of Kotzebue Sound in the Arctic Ocean to drum and chant in the Inuktitut language. Preservation of their ancient culture is a priority for the Inuit.

The Inuit people, along with the closely related Aleuts, make up the largest native population of the Arctic and sub-Arctic regions of Canada, Alaska, Greenland, and extreme eastern Siberia. From the 16th century onward outsiders referred to all the indigenous peoples of the Arctic as "Eskimos," a term that came from the Montagnais, a non-Arctic Native American people from northern Quebec. In 1977 the Arctic peoples officially became known as Inuit ("the people" in the Inuktitut language). In recent decades the Inuit have made important political gains. They now have control over many of their Arctic territories and have considerable autonomy within their homeland, called Nunavut.

Inuit History and Society

The Inuit are descendants of the aboriginal inhabitants of Alaska. Like their ancestors, the early Inuit adapted their lifesyle to the harsh northern climate. The extreme cold prevented them from growing crops or keeping livestock, so they survived by fishing and by hunting caribou and large sea mammals, such as seals, walrus, and whales. As the seasons changed, the Inuit moved from place to place to make use of the best food sources. In the winter they lived on the coast, hunting sea mammals and traveling on sleds pulled by teams of dogs. During the ice-free months they moved inland, on foot or in animal-skin boats called kayaks, to hunt caribou. They also trapped bears and small animals, and caught fish in underwater traps, or weirs.

Because of their nomadic (wandering) lifestyle, the Inuit did not create permanent settlements. If they planned to stay in one area for more than a few days, they constructed houses from whalebone or driftwood and sod. Otherwise, they lived in animal-skin tents in summer or built temporary winter homes called igloos (from the Inuit word *igdlu*, meaning "snow house"). They were dome-shaped dwellings built from blocks of snow, with windows made of ice or animal hide, and a central fire for heating and cooking. The Inuit stayed warm and dry by wearing seal-skin boots and caribou-skin parkas, pants, and mittens. At night they slept on platforms covered with animal skins.

Inuit families consisted of five or six relatives. The women cooked, took care of the home, and raised the children, while the men hunted. Up to 10 families formed a hunting group, choosing a leader based on his ability to take care of them. The Inuit developed peaceful ways of resolving conflicts and rarely went to war with each other. Their tradition of *ningiqtuq*, or sharing, included giving food to elderly people who could not hunt for themselves. This concept of sharing is still an important part of Inuit culture.

Distribution

- Alaska
- Nunavut
- Nunavik (Quebec)
- Newfoundland
- Labrador

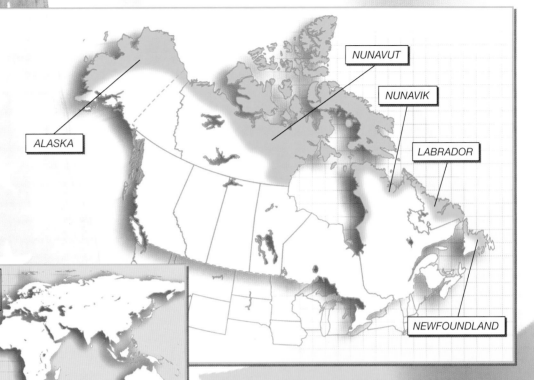

ALASKA

NUNAVUT

NUNAVIK

LABRADOR

NEWFOUNDLAND

Region of origin

Northern Alaska, the Canadian Arctic coast, and Greenland.

Population

55,700 in Canada and an estimated 95,000 more worldwide.

Jobs

Mining, oil and gas, construction, government, administration, hunting, and crafts. Unemployment is a serious problem, but the Nunavut Territory is working to expand its economy and improve job opportunities for its citizens.

Language

The eastern Inuit speak Inuktitut or local dialects such as Kalaallit (Greenland) and Inuvialuit (Canada). The western Inuit speak Inupiat, Yupiget, Yuplit, Alutiit, and Yupik.

Notable Inuit individuals

Kenojuak Ashevak, artist, and winner of the Order of Canada, 1967.
Clare Evelyn Clark, first president of the Indian-Eskimo Association of Canada.
Joseph Idlout, actor.
Emile Immaroitok, Inuktitut language expert and teacher.
Zacharias Kunuk, filmmaker.
Paul Okalik, premier of Nunavut (2002).
Charlie Panigoniak, musician.
Qitdlarssuaq, leader of the last great Inuit migration from Baffin Island to Greenland in the 19th century.
Natar Ungalaaq, actor, filmmaker, and sculptor.

Useful websites

Census information and statistics
(www.statcan.ca/english/census96/jan13/abor4.htm)
(www.statgreen.gl/english/yearbook/chap24.html)
Daily life and current issues
(www.isuma.ca/about_us/arnait/index.html)
(www.kativik.qc.ca/Ulluriaq/Nunavik/inuitlife)
History and general information
(http://collections.ic.gc.ca/arctic/inuit/history.htm)
(www.canadianembassy.org/reference/nunavut.asp)
(www.diversitywatch.ryerson.ca/watch/backgrounds/inuit.html)
(www.ainc-inac.gc.ca/pr/info/info114_e.pdf)
Inuit Circumpolar Conference
(www.inuit.org)
Inuit music
(www.arctictravel.com/chapters/inmusicpage.html)

Religion

Mainly Protestant, with some native shamanistic beliefs.

Festivals

Most festivals are local celebrations of various aspects of Inuit art, culture, or history, often performed to educate non-Inuits.

Food

Whale, caribou, seal, fish, goose, ptarmigan, and other meats, eaten cooked, dried, or frozen; wild fruit and vegetables.

Two Inuit traders sit outside the Golden Gate Store in Nome, Alaska, in 1900. The store sold furs, haberdashery, curios, and general household goods.

Inuit Migrations

From 1000 to 1200 climate change brought slightly warmer conditions to the western Arctic, causing many species of whales to move eastward. The Inuit followed the whales into eastern Canada, and many groups settled near the rich whaling grounds off Baffin and Somerset islands. Some groups settled in coastal areas, developing villages and hunting mainly seals, caribou, and fish.

From 1300 to 1500 the world became progressively colder. This climatic change, called the "Little Ice Age," forced even the tough and adaptable Inuit to move southward, out of the high Arctic.

Inuit Culture

The Inuit had a complex view of the world that was reflected in their art and mythology. Traditional Inuit carvers shaped tusks and bones into figures of people and of the animals that dominated their lives. They believed that animals, along with inanimate objects and forces of nature, had spirits with human characteristics. They also thought that human souls joined the spirit world after death. Religious leaders called shamans helped people communicate with and honor the spirits. They were especially careful not to offend the spirits of the game animals that were so important for their survival. Today, although many of these shamanistic beliefs have been lost, Inuit artists are still deeply influenced by the natural world. They create stone carvings, lithographs, and drawings, and there are galleries in Canada and around the world that specialize in Inuit art.

European Contact and Changing Ways of Life

In 1250 Inuit living in the far northwest of Greenland first encountered medieval Norse hunters, or Vikings, who had colonies in southwest Greenland founded by Eric the Red. These colonies disappeared in the mid-1400s, although historians still do not know why, and meeting the Norse did not have a lasting effect on the Inuit.

The first significant contact with Europeans occurred in the 16th century, with the arrival of explorers looking for the Northwest Passage, a water route through the Arctic that would give them a shortcut from Europe to the spices, silks, and other riches of Asia. Some explorers were hostile and had violent encounters with the Inuit. Others engaged in trade or exchanged gifts. None of them found a northwest passage, but the Inuit learned of the outside world

Inuit Circumpolar Conference

The Inuit Circumpolar Conference (ICC) is an international organization that represents about 150,000 Inuit living in Alaska, Canada, Greenland, and Siberia. The ICC works to strengthen unity among the Inuit, protect Inuit rights and interests internationally, develop Inuit culture, encourage long-term policies to safeguard the environment, and work for the human rights of all indigenous peoples. It holds a General Assembly every four years.

and came to appreciate what it had to offer, especially iron, which the Inuit used to make harpoon points and knife blades.

In the 1850s Europeans and Americans sailed into Canadian waters and set up large-scale whaling and fur-trapping operations. Many Inuit worked on the whaling boats, and they began to buy European goods, from rifles and tent canvas to wooden boats and flour. The fur trade encouraged the Inuit to hunt foxes for their fur. By the early 1920s nearly all Inuit lived within traveling distance of a trading post and had started to form permanent communities.

The whalers also brought infectious diseases to the Inuit. With no natural immunities, the Inuit died by the thousands. The population of western Canadian Arctic Inuit, called the Inuvialuit, dropped from 2,000–2,500 in 1850 to just 150 people in 1910. Another local group of Inuit, the Sadlirmiut of Southampton Island, was completely wiped out by dysentery over the winter of 1902–1903.

By 1905 Arctic whale stocks were running out, and the whaling industry was dying. Between 1918 and 1928 some companies switched their focus to the northern fur trade and moved north into the Arctic. With the traders came Anglican and Roman Catholic missionaries. The influence of these new Christian missionaries meant that many traditional spiritual beliefs of the Inuit died out.

The 20th Century

By the 1920s the Inuit had abandoned many of their traditional beliefs and practices. They had little political power, and instability in the fur trade left many people without a reliable source of income. After World War II (1939–1945) the Canadian government realized that the Inuit were suffering from poverty and sometimes even starvation. The Inuit were encouraged to settle down and form permanent communities so that they could take advantage of social welfare. Government services expanded within the new settlements, bringing housing developments, schools, hospitals, airports, and modern stores. By the mid-1960s most Inuit lived in government settlements. Job opportunities were limited, and many people became dependent on government assistance.

The Transition to Self-Government

In 1966 the Canadian government created federal electoral constituencies in certain parts of the Northwest Territories. The following year a commissioner for the Northwest Territories and a new territorial government were appointed. The 1960s also saw the development of "Eskimo co-ops" in most Arctic settlements. They allowed the Inuit to control sales of their art and helped keep fur prices up and merchandise costs down.

Inuit music

Music, both ancient and modern, is a very important part of Inuit culture. Traditional drum dances can include just a few people or fill a special snow house where people gather to socialize. "Throat singing" is usually performed by two women; each singer repeats a different sound in a fast rhythm, imitating the low-pitched sounds made by birds and animals. Contemporary Inuit musicians, such as Susan Aglukark, the singing duo Tudjaat, Charlie Panigoniak, Simon Sigjariaq, Mary Atuat Thompson, Peter and Susan Aningmiuq, William Tagoona, Colin Adjun, and Itulu Itidlui, are very popular. Many of these artists combine aspects of traditional music with modern instruments. Some Inuit also enjoy listening to mainstream country-and-western music and gospel music on the radio.

An Inuit family at mealtime. The traditional Inuit diet included local game or fish they had caught themselves, and hunting and fishing are still practiced today.

Inuit sculptors traditionally carved figures of people and animals from bone or ivory, but steel tools have allowed modern Inuit artists to extend their craft to stone carving.

The Inuit Brotherhood, now called Inuit Tapirisat of Canada, was established in 1971. This organization studied Inuit culture and land use and determined which areas should be included in a new Inuit homeland. Five years later the creation of a territory called Nunavut ("our land" in Inuktitut) was proposed. The Nunavut Final Agreement was signed in May 1993, and the new territory was proclaimed on April 1, 1999. Nunavut comprises the central and eastern parts of the Northwest Territories and covers 772,000 square miles (2 million square kilometers), or roughly one-fifth of the land area of Canada. Nunavut has its own government, which promotes Inuit culture and rights and is working to build up the territory's economy to help all its residents, whether they are Inuit or not.

The Future of the Inuit

The Inuit of the 21st century face a range of challenges. Economically, the Arctic is still underdeveloped. Job opportunities are scarce, and few people have the education or skills needed to compete for the jobs that do exist. Mining of diamonds, gold, and other heavy metals, as well as gas and oil extraction, may create new jobs, and the growing tourist industry is a potential source of revenue, but social assistance continues to support about a third of the population. Life expectancy among the Inuit is also poor compared to other parts of the world. The Inuit have high rates of infant mortality and nonnatural deaths from injuries, suicides, and murders. There is also a high prevalence of chronic disease, including cancer and diabetes, among the Inuit. However, the Inuit have a young and vibrant population and a long tradition of overcoming obstacles. Their goals are to preserve their culture and to achieve a decent standard of living. Their history of strength and endurance suggests that they will succeed.

Iranians

While highly successful in western society, Iranian Americans have not assimilated, but have worked hard to maintain their unique culture and Farsi language. However, Iranian Americans have also suffered prejudice due to tensions between the United States and Iran and misunderstandings about their Muslim faith.

Iranian immigration to North America closely parallels the political history between Iran and the United States. The two countries developed close ties beginning in 1953, when the U.S. Central Intelligence Agency (CIA) backed an Iranian military coup that restored to power the deposed shah, Mohammed Reza Pahlavi. From the mid-1950s until 1977 tens of thousands of Iranian students entered the United States to pursue higher education courses and to gain technical skills sorely needed by Iran's emerging industries. But the Iranian Revolution (1978–1979) undermined relations between Iran and North America. The revolution toppled the Western-backed government, replacing it with the Islamic Republic of Iran, governed by the laws of the Koran as interpreted by a *faqhi*, or spiritual leader. Currently, Iran is the only theocracy (religious state) in the world.

Iranian Communities in North America

The number of Iranians who entered the United States as nonimmigrants (those without a permanent visa) during the revolution rose dramatically to over 100,000 each year. In the early 1980s an average of more than 10,000 immigrants with permanent visas entered each year. This large influx created thriving Iranian American communities in North America. Many Iranians (up to 35 percent) settled in the greater Los Angeles area.

Iranian Americans are the third most educated immigrant group in the United States. In 1990, 56.2 percent had received bachelor's degrees, 26 percent had graduate degrees, and 90.8 percent had graduated from high school. Iranian Americans are also motivated entrepreneurs: 21 percent are self-employed. Nearly 50 percent have white-collar professional jobs, and many are medical professionals with their own healthcare practices.

Iranian Americans and Cultural Identity

Despite their achievements, Iranian Americans have not been assimilated into North American culture. Instead, they have developed a lasting interest in Iranian culture. Their pride in their traditions, including music, food, and religious celebrations, is highlighted by their use of the Farsi language; while nearly all Iranian Americans are fluent in English, many speak Farsi whenever possible. Iranian Americans often choose to go back to Iran; since 1989 over 100,000 have returned to their homeland.

Iranian Americans have strong political and emotional ties to Iran. These women gathered outside the White House to draw attention to the Iran–Iraq War (1980–1988).

Notable Iranian Americans

Sara Amir, immigrants' and
   women's rights activist.
Vartan Gregorian, president of
   Brown University.
Lotfi Mansouri, Canadian
   theatrical director.
Shardad Rohani, composer
   and conductor.

See also

• Anti-immigrant prejudice
   (Volume 1)
• Assimilation (Volume 1)
• Education (Volume 3)
• Iraqis (Volume 5)
• Kurds (Volume 6)

Religion is a central part of life for Iranian Americans, but Iranians in North America do not represent a typical cross-section of Iranian religions. Iran is nearly 98 percent Muslim, and 93 percent are from the Shi'ite sect. In contrast, besides representing both Shi'ite and Sunni sects of Islam, Iranian Americans also include many Baha'is, Christians, and Jews. The Baha'is in particular have suffered much persecution: Even though their faith originated in Iran as an offshoot of Shi'ism, the Iranian government treats their beliefs as heresy.

Political Conflict and Prejudice

Tensions between the United States and Iran have often made life difficult for Iranian Americans. Beginning with the Iranian Revolution of 1979, when Ayatollah Ruhollah Khomeini seized control of Iran and 52 American hostages were held at the U.S. Embassy in Tehran for 144 days, Americans have taken a dim view of Iranians. During that crisis many Iranians who had fled to the United States were threatened with deportation. Relations have deteriorated again since the extremist Islamic terrorist attacks of September 11, 2001. In January 2002 President George W. Bush identified Iran, Iraq, and North Korea as an "axis of evil," a group of countries whose governments are a threat to world peace by their efforts to acquire weapons of mass destruction.

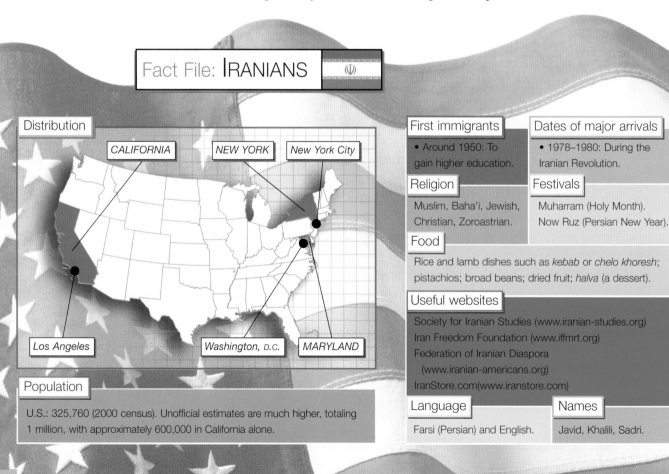

Fact File: IRANIANS

Distribution

CALIFORNIA NEW YORK New York City

Los Angeles Washington, D.C. MARYLAND

Population

U.S.: 325,760 (2000 census). Unofficial estimates are much higher, totaling 1 million, with approximately 600,000 in California alone.

First immigrants

• Around 1950: To gain higher education.

Religion

Muslim, Baha'i, Jewish, Christian, Zoroastrian.

Food

Rice and lamb dishes such as *kebab* or *chelo khoresh*; pistachios; broad beans; dried fruit; *halva* (a dessert).

Dates of major arrivals

• 1978–1980: During the Iranian Revolution.

Festivals

Muharram (Holy Month). Now Ruz (Persian New Year).

Useful websites

Society for Iranian Studies (www.iranian-studies.org)
Iran Freedom Foundation (www.iffmrt.org)
Federation of Iranian Diaspora
   (www.iranian-americans.org)
IranStore.com(www.iranstore.com)

Language

Farsi (Persian) and English.

Names

Javid, Khalili, Sadri.

Iraqis

Iraqi Americans form a small but increasingly significant part of the Arab population in North America. During the 1980s and 1990s Iraqi Muslims accounted for the third-largest increase in Arab immigrants. The 2000 U.S. census reported 34,444 Iraqi Americans, but Iraqi American community members calculate that there are 300,000 Iraqi American Muslims if first-, second-, and third-generation immigrants are included. Iraqi Christians, known as Chaldeans, do not appear on any census data, but their community members estimate they number 60,000 in North America.

Early Immigrants

Iraqi Christians came to the United States as early as 1910. Many settled around Detroit, Michigan, where the auto industry was beginning. The Chaldeans belong to a subgroup of the Roman Catholic church. They accept the doctrines of the Catholic Church, but their religious services differ in ritual order, music, and their use of the Aramaic language. Because of their distinct language and religion Chaldeans see themselves as separate from other Iraqis.

The first Iraqi Muslim immigrants began to enter North America in the 1950s and 1960s. Most were students from wealthy families who entered the United States to pursue higher education. They often stayed in the United States after receiving their degrees. After 1958, when a military coup in Iraq toppled the British-supported monarchy, the resulting political instability led to an increase in the number of Iraqi students seeking citizenship in North America.

Shi'ite and Sunni Muslims

Islam, the dominant religion in Iraq, is divided into the Sunni and Shi'ite sects. In Iraq the two sects are about equal in numbers, and their differences create internal power struggles and economic competition. Iraqi Shi'ites believe that government should be subject to Islamic law and do not support the current secular (nonreligious) Ba'ath Party regime of Saddam Hussein, who came to power in 1968. By the late 1970s the party had begun to persecute everyone who opposed Saddam's rule. Many people fled the country. Approximately 300,000 Shi'ites were deported to Iran, and many traveled from there to the United States. The majority of Iraqi Muslims in North America today are Shi'ites.

Consequences of the Persian Gulf War

Many Iraqis who supported the international coalition against Saddam Hussein's regime during the 1990–1991 Persian Gulf War escaped to other countries after the war. The United States admitted nearly 10,000 Iraqis,

The Persian Gulf War

U.S. Marines in action during Operation Desert Storm in the Persian Gulf War of 1991 (below). On August 1, 1990, Saddam Hussein's Iraqi army invaded the neighboring state of Kuwait to take control of its oilfields. An international alliance led by the United States condemned this act of aggression, and a force of 600,000 ground troops from some 28 nations was assembled to expel the invaders. Following an allied aerial bombardment on enemy positions that lasted more than a month, ground fighting began on February 24, 1991. The conflict lasted five days, at the end of which time U.S and allied forces had achieved a convincing victory, driving the Iraqis out of Kuwait and returning the country to independence. As a result of the war Arab Americans in general and Iraqi Americans in particular suffered from suspicion and prejudice in their everyday lives.

Food

Typical Iraqi foods include *hummus* (a chickpea spread), *falafel* (spicy vegetables, formed into balls and fried), *bistalla* (meat and rice in a pastry), and *baklava* (nuts and honey in thin pastry). Filled pastries are a traditional Iraqi dish and can be made with a variety of ingredients, including cheese, almonds, or dates.

See also

• Education (Volume 3)
• Iranians (Volume 5)
• Kurds (Volume 6)
• National loyalties (Volume 7)

mostly Kurds and Shi'ite Muslims. The strained relations between the United States and Iraq make life difficult for Iraqi Americans. They feel torn between allegiance to their new home and love of their native country. Most Iraqi Americans do not support Saddam's regime, but they also worry that friends and relatives in Iraq are being hurt by the U.S. sanctions (limits on trade) that were set up to punish Iraq for not obeying international law. An unfortunate side effect of the Persian Gulf War (and, more recently, the "war on terrorism," when, in 2002, President George W. Bush identified Iraq as being part of an "axis of evil") has been an increase in prejudice toward and harassment of Iraqi Americans in their day-to-day lives.

Iraqi American Culture

The Iraqi Muslims who came to North America in the 1990s are culturally conservative; they believe in traditions such as arranged marriages and strict child-raising. Both Iraqi Muslims and Iraqi Chaldeans usually have large families, and the divorce rate is very low. Iraqi Americans also place a high value on education. Most newly arrived Iraqis attend "English as a Second Language" classes, and many Iraqi Americans, including an increasing number of women, enroll in college degree courses.

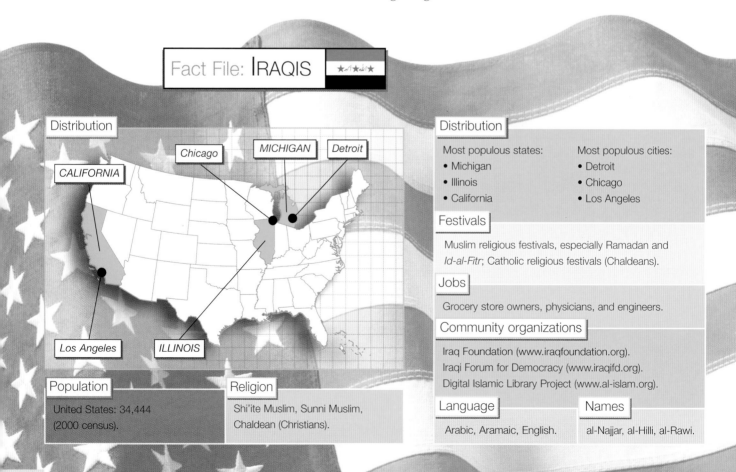

Fact File: IRAQIS

Distribution

Chicago · MICHIGAN · Detroit · CALIFORNIA · Los Angeles · ILLINOIS

Distribution

Most populous states:
• Michigan
• Illinois
• California

Most populous cities:
• Detroit
• Chicago
• Los Angeles

Festivals

Muslim religious festivals, especially Ramadan and *Id-al-Fitr*; Catholic religious festivals (Chaldeans).

Jobs

Grocery store owners, physicians, and engineers.

Community organizations

Iraq Foundation (www.iraqfoundation.org).
Iraqi Forum for Democracy (www.iraqifd.org).
Digital Islamic Library Project (www.al-islam.org).

Population

United States: 34,444 (2000 census).

Religion

Shi'ite Muslim, Sunni Muslim, Chaldean (Christians).

Language

Arabic, Aramaic, English.

Names

al-Najjar, al-Hilli, al-Rawi.

Irish immigrants have had a profound influence on every aspect of American life throughout its history. Today some 33 million people in the United States claim Irish ancestry, according to the 2000 U.S. census, making the Irish the second largest ethnic group in the country. The story of the Irish in America began with the earliest European arrivals and peaked with a disastrous Irish famine in the 1840s, when more than a million people emigrated from Ireland. Though Ireland is currently enjoying the most fruitful period in its economic history, a long history of emigration and a thirst for adventure continue to send thousands of young Irish men and women to the United States and Canada. The Irish have a reputation as a highly motivated, educated, and hard-working people, and people of Irish origin are found at all levels of the American workforce. Irish-born immigrants have a high representation in the trades, in professional and administrative positions, in healthcare, and in the service industries. In cities like New York, Boston, and Chicago the Irish fit in so well that at first glance they are nearly indistinguishable from the larger population.

History of Irish Immigration

The 1636 arrival of the Irish vessel *St. Patrick* in Boston Harbor ignited riots in the city for fear of a Catholic invasion in the primarily English Protestant city. Overriding these religious and social concerns, however, was the dire need for a labor force. So began a steady flow of Irish immigrants to America. Thousands of Irish people were taken on as servants by the English in the mid-1600s. Still more came across the Atlantic as indentured servants, exiled convicts, political and military prisoners, and paying passengers planning to escape the hopeless economic conditions and oppressive British rule at home in Ireland.

During the 1600s Irish immigrants also included a small population of wealthy Irish Catholics, as well as some Irish Protestant descendants of English and Scottish colonialists. Estimates indicate that there were some 350,000 to 400,000 Irish people living in the United States by the outbreak of the American Revolution in 1775. Throughout the colonial and revolutionary years the Irish comprised the largest non-English, non-African group of settlers in America.

Life was hard for the majority of early Irish settlers. Arriving without the special skills or trades needed to make a living, the Irish had to take the low-paid jobs that native-born Americans would not.

A visual interpretation of Ireland's plight in the 19th century, when famine was rampant, and the Irish looked to the United States as a place of refuge and hope.

Irish clam diggers on the dockside in Boston, Massachusetts, in 1882. Boston remains the home of one of the United States' largest Irish American communities.

Fact File: IRISH

Distribution

Most populous states:
- Massachusetts
- New Hampshire
- Rhode Island
- Pennsylvania
- Missouri

Most populous cities:
- Boston
- New York
- Chicago
- Philadelphia

MASSACHUSETTS NEW HAMPSHIRE

New York City

Chicago

MISSOURI

PENNSYLVANIA

RHODE ISLAND

Boston

Philadelphia

Region of origin

Ireland

The island of Ireland lies to the west of Britain in the North Atlantic.

Population

U.S.: 33 million (2000 census);
Canada: 3,767,610 (1996 census).

Language

English, with a small percentage of Irish Gaelic speakers.

Useful websites

Irish American Heritage Center (www.irishamhc.com)
Irish American Information Service (www.iais.org)
Irish to America 1846-1886 (http://home.att.net/~wee-monster/irish.html)
The Irish Abroad (www.irishabroad.com)
The Irish in America (www.irishinamerica.net)
The Irish in America (www.pbs.org/wgbh/pages/irish)
The U.S.-Ireland Alliance (www.us-irelandalliance.org)

Community organizations

The Ancient Order of Hibernians
A Catholic, Irish American fraternal organization
    (http://community.cleveland.com/cc/aohboland-berry)
Emerald Society of the Boston Police
One of the first police Emerald Societies formed in the United
    States (http://Bosemsoc.PoliceOfficer.com)
The Erin Go Bragh Foundation
    Nonprofit organization dedicated to establishing an Irish
    American heritage museum (www.eringobragh.net)
Baltimore Irish Network (www.baltimoreirish.net/iorg.htm)

Jobs

Legal immigrants can be found in various professions at all levels of the occupational scale. They include banking, computing, medicine, and other professional positions. Illegal immigrants are more likely to work as laborers or in childcare.

First immigrants

Edward Nugent, serving with Captain Ralph Lane in 1586, reputedly killed the Indian chief Pemispan in North Carolina. Two Irishmen named Darbie Glaven and Dennis Carrell served with Captain John White in Virginia in 1587.

Festivals

Saint Patrick's Day (March 17).
Christmas Day (December 25)
Saint Stephen's Day (December 26)
All major Catholic festivals.

Food

Varies widely. A common description of dinner is "meat, potatoes, and two veg." Smoked bacon, beef, ham, lamb, turkey, cabbage, potatoes, turnip, and carrots are traditional fare of Irish-born people. Irish people tend to prefer tea to coffee. Guinness stout is a favorite Irish-made beer.

Names

Typical Irish surnames are Donahue, Donegan, Flaherty, Flynn, Kennedy, Kelly, Nevin, O'Connor, O'Rourke, Murphy, and Ryan.

Many of the earliest arrivals came as indentured servants, and even by the mid-19th century the situation had barely improved. The immigrants were typically unskilled and regarded as cheap day labor. Lacking means for an adequate income, many lived a miserable life in slum apartments in dockside areas. The arrival of huge numbers of poverty-stricken immigrants aroused intense anti-Irish feeling, and from the mid-1800s the Irish became one of the first groups to face widespread prejudice in America. "No Irish Need Apply" signs became common at many places of employment across the country.

However, the Irish contribution to the Revolutionary War (1775–1783) won them respect as loyal Americans, and they began to take the lead in local politics and labor movements during the late 1700s and 1800s. The Irish contributed to the trade union movement through groups such as the Molly Maguires—Pennsylvania coal miners who organized unions during the 1860s and 1870s. In the late 1800s the New York Irish political organization, Tammany Hall, dominated local urban politics.

The Great Famine Migration

The failure of Irish potato crops from the 1820s through 1847 led to widespread famine and disease in Ireland. Few options remained: emigrate or die. Between 1845 and 1851 the population of Ireland dropped by about two million, half due to emigration and half to starvation and disease. From 1820 to 1920 some 4.7 million Irish people emigrated to the United States. Most were unskilled workers from the hard-hit rural areas of western Ireland.

In 1890 the Irish-born population in the United States was 1.8 million. These immigrants settled and had families, and by 1920 the second-generation Irish population exceeded three million, outnumbering first-generation Irish by three to one. With a growing population of fully assimilated and increasingly affluent second-generation Irish Americans, the Irish began a slow climb up the social ladder. This transformation was helped by an effective Catholic school system.

The Making of Irish America

The next wave of Irish emigration came in the 1920s. A failed 1916 rebellion against British rule in Ireland ignited a war that resulted in independence in 1921. Then a civil war and a drop in farm prices left many with no means to make a living. Again, many moved to North America in search of a better way of life. Immigrants arrived to find a thriving Irish community. Irish people by this time held significant positions of political power and had helped shape political life, playing a leadership role in developing its labor structures and trade unions.

Michael Flatley

Michael Flatley, dancer, flautist, and choreographer, was the star of major Broadway shows *Riverdance* and *Lord of the Dance*. Born to Irish parents in Chicago, he was taught respect for Irish culture from an early age. At the age of 11 he enrolled in Irish step-dancing classes and quickly excelled at the traditional dance style—straight torso above fast-moving feet. By the time he reached 17 he was the first American All-World Champion in Irish dancing. His Broadway shows were wildly popular globally for their contemporary combination of traditional Irish step dancing and modern dance forms. Flatley (below, with Jean Butler) is largely responsible for bringing traditional Irish music and dance to a worldwide audience.

Irish emigrants pay their passage money at the emigration agent's office in Cork, Ireland, in 1851, before setting off for a new life in North America.

President John F. Kennedy pictured in the White House in 1963, a few months before he was assassinated in Dallas, Texas. Kennedy became the first Irish American Catholic president and the youngest man ever to hold the office when he was inaugurated in 1961 aged 43.

During the Great Depression of the 1930s Irish immigration dropped to a trickle, though it regained strength after World War II (1939–1945). The war had wreaked havoc on Ireland's economy, starting another tide of emigration that continued through the 1950s. The U.S. Immigration and Nationality Act of 1952, which allowed unrestricted immigration from the Western Hemisphere, brought another large influx of Irish to the United States. However, by the 1950s the number of second-generation Irish far outnumbered the Irish-born by four to one.

About 400,000 Irish people emigrated during the 1950s. It was the highest rate of emigration since the famine migrations. Between 1951 and 1961, 34,155 Irish people came to the United States and Canada. This wave lasted until 1965, when a new U.S. Immigration and Nationality Act put a virtual end to immigration.

The next large immigration was in the 1980s. The U.S. government instituted three major laws that gave the Irish increased access to legal immigration. Documented Irish immigration went up from 902 in 1981 to 10,000 in 1990, but it is estimated that there are now about 150,000 illegal Irish immigrants living in cities along the eastern seaboard from Boston to Philadelphia. By the 1990s, as part of an economic boom called "the Celtic Tiger," jobs in Ireland were plentiful—especially high-tech jobs. However, with the failure of the "dotcom" internet industry in 2001, many jobs were lost, and Irish emigration to North America began to increase once more.

Irish Communities Today

The Irish were no longer ostracized as a minority immigrant community in the United States by the beginning of the 20th century. By 1960 the Irish Americans could claim the first Catholic president of the United States, John Fitzgerald Kennedy. Kennedy's election symbolized the American dream for many Irish Americans, showing just how much an Irish immigrant family could achieve in building a new life in the United States.

Irish communities in America are held together by a variety of political and labor organizations, community clubs, charitable societies, religious organizations, and cultural activities such as sports and musical events. Younger Irish people in America socialize at Irish pubs, which are numerous. Older generations often belong to Irish cultural organizations and clubs formed around shared geographical origins in the home country. Most major cities have nonprofit Irish immigration centers dedicated to serving the housing, employment, legal, and social needs of new Irish immigrants.

Irish Americans are distributed throughout rural, suburban, and urban areas, though most new arrivals tend to live in the cities, where jobs are more plentiful, and where there is a larger and more well-established Irish community. Boston and New York are the most popular destinations, while Chicago, Philadelphia, and San Francisco also have significant Irish populations. Almost all Irish people speak English. A small percentage of people from western, rural parts of Ireland speak Irish Gaelic. Only 0.5 percent of Irish people living in United States do not speak English well.

Irish Americans enjoy a high standard of living. The 1990 U.S. census reports a mean household income of $40,358. Of these people, 62 percent work in professional and clerical positions, 12 percent in service industries, and 26 percent in labor-related positions. The large majority of people of Irish ancestry in the United States live in single-family households, and 67 percent own their own homes.

There is an important distinction between Irish Americans and new Irish immigrants. Only 1.2 percent of all people claiming Irish ancestry in the United States were born in Ireland. Within this 1.2 percent, 82 percent arrived before 1980. Because the Irish assimilate so well into American culture—indeed, they played a major role in helping shape its culture throughout history—Irish people tend to mix freely among Irish Americans and other Americans at work, at home, and in social settings. New immigrants adhere more closely to Irish values of family and community, and tend to socialize and find work through Irish networks.

Education, Religion, and Politics

Ireland, dubbed "the Land of Saints and Scholars," holds both church and education in high regard. Most Irish immigrants are Catholic, although a smaller community of Irish people are Protestant. Historically, Irish life in America centered around the church and parish activities. However, today the church's role has receded in the lives of many Irish people, and some only attend Catholic mass at Christmas

Notable Irish Americans

Daniel Boone, pioneer.
William Frederick "Buffalo Bill" Cody, frontiersman and showbusiness entrepreneur.
Davy Crockett, pioneer.
Michael Flatley, dancer, flautist, and choreographer.
Jackie Gleason, comedian and actor.
Gene Kelly, dancer, singer, and actor.
John F. Kennedy, the first Catholic president of the United States (1960–1963).
Frank McCourt, author of best-selling novel *Angela's Ashes*.
Maureen O'Hara, actress.
Ronald Reagan (seen below with his wife Nancy and Pope John Paul II), actor and U.S. president (1981–1989).
John Wayne, movie actor.

and Easter, and for important family and social milestones such as weddings, christenings, and funerals.

People of Irish ancestry in the United States are an educated group. About 80 percent have completed a high school degree or higher; 21.2 percent have completed a bachelor's degree or higher; 7.2 percent have completed a graduate degree. The Irish founded some of the most prestigious universities in the United States, including Boston College, Notre Dame, Georgetown University, and Holy Cross. Notre Dame's football team is nicknamed "the Fighting Irish," and their logo portrays a leprechaun with fists raised.

The Irish in American Politics

The Irish have also made significant gains in social status through politics. Some say that the Irish "invented" urban politics. At the beginning of the 20th century, and for a good part of it, Irish dominance in U.S. city wards—the most localized unit of city politics, which operated much like Catholic parishes might have in Ireland—provided the Irish with a foot in the door to the middle class. Residents in need of, for example, a job, housing, or a liquor license would appeal to the ward boss, whose votes were secured by his service to his community. Indeed, much of the history of U.S. politics included people of Irish ancestry. Nine of the signatories of the Declaration of Independence were of Irish origin, and 19 U.S. presidents have claimed Irish heritage, including George Washington, John F. Kennedy, and Ronald Reagan. The Irish have a high rate of citizenship in the United States. Some 64 percent of documented, foreign-born Irish people are naturalized, voting citizens. However, they remain supportive of many causes in Ireland, particularly those related to "the Troubles," an extended struggle over political dominance of Northern Ireland, which is under British rule. This often violent period of civil and political unrest between nationalist (primarily Catholic) and loyalist (primarily Protestant) communities is a hotly contested, emotional topic. Numerous Irish groups in America send money and other support to Northern Ireland, with varying objectives. For example, the American Ireland Fund has raised more than $100 million for peace and cultural projects since the 1980s. Politicians with Irish ancestry have been particularly supportive and active in pursuing a peace process in Northern Ireland in recent years.

A player takes a free shot from the 21-yard line during a game of "hurling" at New York's Croke Park. The traditional Irish game of hurling is a fast and furious sport played by two teams of 15 men who score points by running, hitting, or bouncing a ball called a "sliotar" into goals using a paddle-like stick called a "hurley."

Participants in a Saint Patrick's Day parade in Boston, Massachusetts. College students ride a float through the streets of South Boston, a traditionally Irish neighborhood. Perhaps the most famous Saint Patrick's Day parade is the one held in New York City.

Irish Culture in North America

Radio, cable television, and ethnic newspapers form an important link to the home country. Newspapers from Ireland are readily available in large North American cities. Numerous local Irish American newspapers, such as *The Irish Emigrant*, *The Irish Voice*, and *The Irish Echo*, combine news of Ireland and of the Irish American community. These publications also include listings of social events, concerts, and fundraising events.

Music is important to the Irish. Many Irish Americans introduce their children to Irish culture by enrolling them in the Irish step-dancing and traditional music schools that abound in Irish communities. Some communities hold an annual *fleadh cheoil* (the Irish Gaelic term for "music festival"), bringing together dance troupes and musicians from many towns in competition. Irish festivals usually also include touring music groups from Ireland, as well as vendors selling Irish goods and services. Many Irish Americans also learn about their own ethnic identity and history through the stories told in popular Irish folk ballads.

The most prominent celebration of Irish culture is Saint Patrick's Day (March 17), which is celebrated with parades in major cities, a traditional meal of corned beef and cabbage (though this is an American tradition; most Irish nationals say that they have never had corned beef), and the wearing of green as a symbol of Irish pride. Once a religious festival, Saint Patrick's Day is now a secular holiday. Alcohol consumption and Irish music are conspicuous parts of the celebration in the United States, but for the Irish the pub is much more than a place to drink beer. It is a center of social life, where people meet, where business is conducted, and where new arrivals get in touch with the Irish network to find housing, jobs, and friends.

See Also

- Anti-immigrant prejudice (Volume 1)
- Assimilation (Volume 1)
- Cultural retention (Volume 3)
- Festivals (Volume 4)
- Immigrant experience (Volume 5)
- Industry and employment (Volume 5)
- Labor unions (Volume 6)
- National politics, U.S. (Volume 7)
- Religion (Volume 9)
- Scotch-Irish (Volume 9)
- Social mobility and race (Volume 9)

Glossary

affirmative action government programs to provide equal opportunities to minority groups.

alien a foreign-born resident who has not been naturalized and is still a subject or citizen of another country.

assimilation the process by which an individual or a minority group adopts the values and practices of the dominant culture and loses its own cultural distinctiveness.

asylum the legal status granted to a foreign individual who fears political persecution if he or she is forced to return home.

bilingualism the ability to speak fluently in two languages.

census a comprehensive survey of a population designed to gather basic demographic information. In the United States the census is carried out every 10 years.

citizen a native or foreign-born member of a country who has legal and political rights within that country.

colony a territory ruled by another country.

cultural mingling a process that occurs when two or more cultures come into contact and interact with one another.

cultural retention the process by which an immigrant group or individual retains elements of their native heritage in a new society.

deportation the legal removal of an immigrant from a country.

diaspora the historical dispersal of a group of people of similar origins from their homeland to many lands.

discrimination the unfair denial of equal rights or opportunities to a group or individual based on cultural, social, or racial differences.

emigrant a person who leaves his or her homeland to live in a foreign country.

emigration the movement of people from their homeland to another country.

emigré a person forced to emigrate for political reasons.

ethnic group a group sharing common origins and cultural similarities, such as beliefs, values, customs, and language, geography, kinship, or race.

ethnicity identification with and inclusion within an ethnic group.

exclusion act a law passed to refuse entry into the United States to a certain race or nationality.

ghetto an often deprived urban area occupied predominantly by members of a single race or ethnic group.

immigrant a person who moves to a country other than his or her homeland.

immigration the settlement of people in a country other than that in which they were born.

indigenous a term referring to the original inhabitants of a land or territory.

integration the mixing of different racial groups within a community.

melting pot a phrase coined by Jewish playwright Israel Zangwill to refer to America's multicultural society in the early 20th century.

middle class a socioeconomic class broadly defined as those with middle income working in mental rather than manual occupations.

migrant a term describing someone who regularly moves from one place to another, often for economic reasons.

migration the movement of people from one country to settle in another.

minority group a subgroup of society characterized by factors including race, religion, nationality, gender, or culture.

multiethnic a term meaning belonging not to one single racial or ethnic group but to two or more.

multiculturalism a positive attitude toward cultural diversity that supports the right of ethnic groups to maintain their cultural distinctiveness within the dominant culture.

nativism an anti-immigrant U.S. political tradition, popular in the 19th century, that valued "real" Americans and their attitudes over more recent immigrants.

naturalization the legal process by which a foreign person becomes a citizen of a country with the same rights as a native-born citizen.

pluralism the equal coexistence of diverse ethnic groups within a single society.

prejudice the holding of unfounded ideas about groups or individuals based on negative stereotypes.

quota (system) a limit on the number of immigrants from particular countries allowed into another.

race the classification of people based on genetic characteristics or common nationality, history, or experiences.

racism discrimination against others based on an assumption of one's own racial superiority.

refugee a term referring to a person who lives in a foreign country to escape persecution at home.

repatriation the forcible or voluntary return of immigrants to their country of origin.

segregation the discriminatory separation or isolation of ethnic, social, or religious groups, for example, in restricted areas such as ghettos.

slavery the ownership of human beings by others.

social mobility the movement of groups or individuals within the social hierachy.

stereotype a usually negative categorization of all individuals within a group based on a rigid and inflexible image of the characteristics of that group.

upper class the more affluent members of society, especially those who have great wealth or hold an esteemed position in society.

urban renewal the rebuilding of deteriorating city neighborhoods, often those that have become ghettos.

working class a social group made up broadly of people in manual occupations.

Ansari, Maboud. *The Making of the Iranian Community in America.* New York: Pardis Press, 1993.

Avery, Donald. *Reluctant Host: Canada's Response to Immigrant Workers 1896–1994.* Toronto: McClelland & Stewart, 1995.

Axtell, James. *Natives and Newcomers: The Cultural Origins of North America.* New York: Oxford University Press, 2000.

Barry, Brian M. *Culture and Equality: An Egalitarian Critique of Multiculturalism.* Cambridge, MA: Harvard University Press, 2001.

Bodnar, John. *The Transplanted: A History of Immigrants in Urban America (Interdisciplinary Studies in History).* Bloomington, IN: Indiana University Press, 1987.

Brown, Dee Alexander. *Bury My Heart at Wounded Knee: An Indian History of the American West.* New York: Henry Holt and Company, 2001 revised edition.

Capp, Diana White Horse. *Brother against Brother: America's New War over Land Rights.* Bellevue, WA: Merril Press, 2002.

Chavez, Leo R. *Shadowed Lives: Undocumented Immigrants in American Society.* Belmont, CA: Wadsworth Pub, 1997.

Ciongoli, A. Kenneth, and Jay Parini. *Passage to Liberty: The Story of Italian Immigration and the Rebirth of America.* New York: Regan Books, HarperCollins, 2002.

Connell-Szasz, Margaret (ed.). *Between Indian and White Worlds: The Cultural Broker.* Norman, OK: University of Oklahoma Press, 1994.

Daniel Tatum, Beverly. *Assimilation Blues: Black Families in a White Community.* Boulder, CO: Basic Books, 2000.

Dezell, Maureen. *Irish America: Coming into Clover.* New York: Doubleday, 2001.

Diner, Hasia R. *Jewish Americans: The Immigrant Experience.* Southport, CT: Hugh Lauter Levin Assoc., 2002.

Do, Hien Duc. *The Vietnamese Americans.* Westport, CT: Greenwood Press, 2000.

Flores, Juan. *Divided Borders: Essays on Puerto Rican Identity.* Houston, TX: Arte Publico Press, 1993.

Franklin, John Hope, and Alfred A. Moss. *From Slavery to Freedom: A History of African Americans.* New York: Alfred A. Knopf, 2000.

Frye Jacobson, Matthew. *Whiteness of a Different Color: European Immigrants and the Alchemy of Race.* Cambridge, MA: Harvard University Press, 1999.

Getis, Arthur, Judith Getis, and I. E. Quastler (eds.). *The United States and Canada: The Land and the People.* New York: McGraw-Hill, 2000.

Gonzalez, Juan. *Harvest of Empire: A History of Latinos in America.* New York: Viking Press, 2000.

Gonzalez-Pando, Miguel. *The Cuban Americans.* Westport, CT: Greenwood Press, 1998.

Govorchin, Gerald Gilbert. *From Russia to America with Love: A Study of the Russian Immigrants in the United States.* Pittsburgh, PA: Dorrance Publishing, 1993.

Grimes, Kimberly M. *Crossing Borders: Changing Social Identities in Southern Mexico.* Tucson, AZ: University of Arizona Press, 1998.

Hegi, Ursula. *Tearing the Silence: Being German in America.* New York: Simon & Schuster, 1997.

Hilfiker, David. *Urban Injustice: How Ghettos Happen.* New York: Seven Stories Press, 2002.

Horn, Michiel. *Becoming Canadian: Memoirs of an Invisible Immigrant.* Toronto: University of Toronto Press, 1997.

Inada, Lawson Fusao (ed.). *Only What We Could Carry: The Japanese American Internment Experience.* Berkeley, CA: Heyday Books, 2000.

Kelley, Ninette, and Michael J. Trebilcock. *The Making of the Mosaic: The History of Canadian Immigration Policy.* Toronto: University of Toronto Press, 1998.

Kelly, Paul. *Multiculturalism Reconsidered: Culture and Equality and Its Critics.* Cambridge, England: Polity Press, 2003.

Kibria, Nazli. *Becoming Asian American: Second-Generation Chinese and Korean American Identities.* Baltimore, MD: Johns Hopkins University Press, 2002.

Lehman, Jeffrey (ed.). *Gale Encyclopedia of Multicultural America.* Detroit, MI: Gale Research, Inc., 2000.

Miscevic, Dusanka, and Peter Kwong. *Chinese Americans: The Immigrant Experience.* Southport, CT: Hugh Lauter Levin Assoc., 2000.

Morton Coan, Peter. *Ellis Island Interviews: In Their Own Words.* New York: Facts on File, 1997.

Naff, Alixa. *The Arab Americans.* Broomall, PA: Chelsea House, 1998.

Portes, Alejandro, and Rubén G. Rumbaut (eds.). *Ethnicities: Children of Immigrants in America.* Los Angeles, CA: University of California Press, 2001.

Stoffman, Daniel. *Who Gets In: What's Wrong with Canada's Immigration Program—And How to Fix It.* Toronto: Macfarlane Walter & Ross, 2002.

Takaki, Ronald. *Strangers from a Different Shore: A History of Asian Americans.* New York: Back Bay Books, 1998.

Thernstrom, Stephan A., Ann Orlov, and Oscar Handlin (eds.). *Harvard Encyclopedia of American Ethnic Groups.* Cambridge, MA: Belknap Press, 1980.

Waldinger, Roger (ed.). *Strangers at the Gates: New Immigrants in Urban America.* Los Angeles, CA: University of California Press, 2001.

Winks, Robin W. *The Blacks in Canada: A History.* Montreal: McGill-Queens University Press, 1997.

Relevant websites are listed separately with each entry.

Immigration timeline

1492 Christopher Columbus sails to North America

1534 Jacques Cartier sails up the St. Lawrence River

1535 Spain establishes colonial government in Mexico

1607 Settlers from England establish a colony in Jamestown, Virginia

1776 Declaration of Independence

1795 Naturalization Act restricts U.S. citizenship to "free white males" who reside in the United States for five years

1798 Alien and Sedition Act allows deportation of "dangerous" foreigners. Naturalization Act increases the residency requirement to 14 years

1802 Congress reduces residency requirement from 14 years to four

1808 Congress bans importation of slaves

1819 Steerage Acts: data collected on immigration for the first time

1820 Chinese arrive in California

1830 Indian Removal Act forces Native Americans to give up their lands east of the Mississippi River

1834 Slavery abolished in British North America (Canada)

1840s Major immigration of Irish and Germans due to crop failures

1846 Mexican–American War starts

1848 Mexican–American War ends. United States purchases New Mexico, Arizona, California, Utah, Nevada, and Texas

1850 Fugitive Slave Act

1860s Mass immigration from Poland

1861 American Civil War begins

1862 American Homestead Act provides settlers with free land in the Midwest

1863 Emancipation Proclamation frees slaves in Union-held territory

1865 American Civil War ends; all slaves freed

1868 The Fourteenth Amendment endows slaves with citizenship. Japanese laborers arrive in Hawaii

1870 The Fifteenth Amendment: African American males given the right to vote

1880s Mass immigration from Italy. Civil unrest and economic instability throughout Russia

1882 Chinese Exclusion Act

1887 The Dawes Act dissolves many Indian reservations in United States

1890s Start of mass immigration of Ukrainians to Canada

1891 Polygamists, the sick, and those convicted of "moral turpitude" made ineligible for immigration

1892 Ellis Island opens

1896 Supreme Court rules that "separate but equal" facilities for blacks and whites are constitutional

1898 The Spanish–American War begins. U.S. acquisition of Puerto Rico and Guam

1900 Jones Act grants U.S. citizenship to Puerto Ricans

1901 Anarchist Exclusion Act

1907 Expatriation Act. "Gentleman's Agreement" curtails Japanese immigration

1910 Mexican Revolution begins: thousands of Mexicans flee to the United States

1917 The United States enters World War I

1918 World War I ends

1921 Quota Act restricts the immigration of southern and eastern Europeans

1924 Johnson–Reed Act reduces fixed quota to 2 percent of nationality groups. Oriental Exclusion Act limits immigration from East Asia. U.S. Border Control created

1929 Congress makes annual immigration quotas permanent

1930s Mass deportation of Mexicans during the Great Depression

1939 World War II begins

1940 Alien Registration Act requires registration and fingerprinting of aliens

1942 Japanese Americans moved to "relocation camps." Bracero Program allows Mexican laborers to work in the United States

1943 Magnuson Act repeals Chinese Exclusion Act of 1882

1945 World War II ends.

1948 Displaced Persons Act permits European war refugees entry to the United States

1950 Internal Security Act bars entry of communists to the United States. Korean War begins

1952 McCarran–Walter Immigration Act removes race as a basis for exclusion

1953 Congress amends the 1948 refugee policy to admit more refugees. Korean War ends

1954 U.S. Supreme Court rules that "separate but equal" educational facilities are unconstitutional. Operation Wetback: INS deports more than 3 million people of Mexican heritage

1959 Cuban revolution

1962 Amendments to Canada's Immigration Act eliminate racial and religious discrimination

1964 Civil Rights Acts

1965 Immigration Act ends quota system. Bracero Program ends. Vietnam War begins

1966 Cuban Refugee Act admits more than 400,000 people to the United States

1971 Canadian government officially endorses policy of multiculturalism

1975 Vietnam War ends: mass immigration from Vietnam

1980 Refugee Act: 10 million permanent immigrants are legally admitted to the United States

1986 The Immigration Reform and Control Act (IRCA) raises annual immigration ceiling to 540,000

1990 Immigration Act allows 700,000 immigrants per year into the United States

1991 Persian Gulf War

1995 Canada officially endorses policy of First Nations self-government

1996 Immigration Act mandates the building of fences on U.S.–Mexico border

2002 Department of Homeland Security established

2003 U.S. forces attack Iraq

Picture credits

Front cover: Corbis: Bettmann; **background image: Corbis:** Bettmann. **Corbis:** 18, 52; Lucien Aigner 24; Tony Arruza 9; Dave Bartruff 54; Nathan Benn 7; Bettmann 21, 32t, 32b, 33, 37, 39, 42t, 42b, 44, 49, 50, 56; Richard A. Cooke 57; Kevin Fleming 26; Owen Franken 48t; Philip Gould 13, 34; Jeff Hunter 14; M. Jackson 47; Wolfgang Kaehler 58; Barry Lewis 25; Christine Osborne 45; Phil Schermeister 12; Leif Skoogfors 59; Ted Spiegel 69; Vince Steano 10; David & Peter Turnley 35; David H. Wells 20; Michael S. Yamashita 38; **Getty Images:** 23, 41, 68; Illustrated London News 66t; Jack Robinson 51; Doreen Spooner 48b; Stock Montage 40; **Library of Congress:** 63t; **National Archives:** 63b; John Fitzgerald Kennedy Library 66b; Ronald Reagan Library 67; **Photos12.com:** Collection Cinema 53; **Rex Features:** Jeremy Sutton-Hibbert 4; Greg Williams 65; **Robert Hunt Library:** 19, 31; **Still Pictures:** Nigel Dickinson 16; **Topham:** Image Works 36; **U.S. Customs Service:** James R. Tourtelotte 29, 30; **U.S. Defense Visual Information Center:** 61.